SO-BSN-561

220.609
B47

133337

DATE DUE			

WITHDRAWN

The Bible in the Churches

How Different Christians Interpret the Scriptures

by
Kenneth Hagen
Daniel J. Harrington, S.J.
Grant R. Osborne
Joseph A. Burgess

CARL A. RUDISILL LIBRARY
LENOIR RHYNE COLLEGE

paulist press *new york/mahwah*

220.609
B47
133337
Sept. 1985

Copyright © 1985 by Joseph Anders Burgess, Daniel Harrington, Grant Osborne, and Kenneth Hagen

All rights reserved. No part of this book may be reproduced or transmitted in any form or by any means, electronic or mechanical, including photocopying, recording, or by any information storage and retrieval system without permission in writing from the publisher.

Library of Congress
Catalog Card Number: 84-62471

ISBN: 0-8091-2676-1

Published by Paulist Press
997 Macarthur Boulevard
Mahwah, N.J. 07430

Printed and bound in the United States of America

Contents

Kenneth Hagen
  Preface   1

Kenneth Hagen
  The History of Scripture in the Church   3

Daniel J. Harrington, S.J.
  Catholic Interpretation of Scripture   35

Grant R. Osborne
  Evangelical Interpretation of Scripture   74

Joseph A. Burgess
  Lutheran Interpretation of Scripture 110

Daniel J. Harrington, S.J.
  Conclusion: Convergence and Divergence 144

could not be exhausted by a literal reading. The early church on up to the discovery of Aristotle was influenced by Platonic philosophy. In Platonic philosophy the particular thing (in Scripture, the letter of the text) is a mirror of reality. The reality is the fuller meaning. As the monk reads Scripture, he finds shades of meaning far beyond what first meets the eye.

"The letter kills, but the Spirit gives life" (2 Cor 3:6) was the New Testament warrant for the Fathers and the monks to distinguish between the literal and the spiritual meaning. The New Testament itself, in its interpretation of the Old, distinguishes between the literal and spiritual meaning. The pattern for interpreting Scripture is contained within Scripture. Interpreting Scripture meant explicating the spiritual depths of meaning. For us, interpretation means bridging the gap between an ancient text and the modern world. When there is only one world there is no separation. So interpretation meant commenting, annotating, explaining the various levels of meaning the Spirit leads one to see.

The most famous form of the multi-level approach became the *quadriga,* the fourfold sense: the literal tells what happened (historical sense), the allegorical teaches what is to be believed, the tropological or moral what is to be done, and the anagogical where it is going or "tending." The usual example was Jerusalem, which refers literally to the city, allegorically to the church, tropologically to the soul, and anagogically to heaven. The monks put this to rhyme. The point is that the letter is a mirror of the almost limitless depth of meaning.

3. The key figure here is Augustine. Augustine pulls together the various strands of patristic exegesis and is the pillar on which the medieval period is built, thus the most important theologian for the entire (thousand year plus) medieval period and on into the sixteenth century. Let us look at how Augustine puts Scripture together, his understanding of Scripture.

Augustine, as is typical throughout this period, sees two eras of salvation represented by the two books of Scripture. The Old Testament and the New Testament represent the old era of salvation and the new era of salvation. The point is that God has a plan for his people, for his creation; and he gives revelation progressively as the people are prepared and able to accept what it is that God has in mind. So there is a progressive revelation going on in Scripture. The ages of Scripture correspond to a person growing up; corporately it is the human race growing up. In the Old Testament the human race is in its infancy or in adolescence, and only as the human race (Israel) became more mature was it ready to receive Christ and the higher revelation. By implication then the fuller understanding of revelation continues in the church.

Another term that Augustine uses is that God is the doctor of medicine and is healing his people. That is what salvation is: health. That is the goal of this creation, revelation, and finally salvation: final healing. So God the doctor prescribes medicine to the extent that the people will respond and grow unto Christ, who is both the physician and the medicine. Christ is the cure as well as the curer. And that continues on through the life of the church. So as Augustine looks at Scripture, he sees God's plan, God's providence. He sees two eras of this plan, and in these two eras God is the doctor healing his people.

Augustine also deals with the Scriptures as books. As a theologian he has the Jewish and Christian manuscripts or books to integrate. A great deal of early hermeneutical effort was spent on the relationship between the two great Testaments. Very generally, the New was considered to be the fulfillment of the Old. Augustine emphasized that what was hidden or veiled in the Old was revealed or uncovered in the New. What was prefigured in the Old was made clear in the New. This is a "both . . . and" relationship, thus the necessity of both Testaments: the New is concealed in the Old, and the Old is made clear in the New. Since the Holy Spirit is the author of both, there is unity and harmony between them. The unity of the Testaments and the progress of revelation is the basis of holding that the New Testament is superior to the Old Testament. The New is new in relation to the Old, and vice versa. Both are needed. The New is more excellent.

So Augustine looks at the Bible in terms of salvation-medicine and healing. He looks at the Bible as a theologian and sees a unity geared toward the superiority of the New Testament as the fulfillment of the Jewish Scriptures. Third, when Augustine looks at Scripture, he sees the two Testaments as two ways of salvation; he sees the two Testaments as two types of people. This is another level on which he looks at Scripture and sees that there is not only that chronological development of the whole race and the whole doctrine, but that there is also the situation that some people of faith back in the Old Testament were actually living ahead of themselves. They were living in the New Testament because they believed Christian doctrine. And he says that in New Testament times there were people who had not seen the message and were still living in the Old Testament because they were living according to the flesh and not according to the Spirit. This is again Augustine's famous letter-Spirit dichotomy, and it becomes an important hermeneutical tool throughout the medieval period on up into modern times. You live according to the letter, or you live according to the Spirit. "The letter kills; the Spirit gives life." So if you live according to the letter, according to the desires of the flesh, you are Old Testament. It does not matter when you live, chronologically speaking, but soteriologically speaking you are old, Augustine says. Or if you live according to the Spirit and you see the Spirit in the letter of Scripture and can see through the veil to the pure light of Christ and Christian doctrine, then you belong to the New Testament and you are new, no matter whether you are Abraham or someone in the New Testament or someone today. So, on balance, what we have from Augustine is a fairly complicated view of Scripture, a multi-nuanced view of Scripture; and it is these various strands of putting Scripture together and interpreting Scripture that continue on through the medieval period.

In between the early period and the high period of the Middle Ages is something of a transitional period from the abbey of Saint Victor in Paris, namely the Victorines. In going from Augustine to Thomas Aquinas via these Victorines, we see that something of hermeneutical shift is underway, a shift that is purported to be developed in Thomas Aquinas. The important thing about the Victorines is that some of them were oriented toward the literal sense of Scripture, toward the historical sense, and used Jewish exegesis for the understanding of the Old Testament. What we had in the Victorines was not so much a theoretical change; that is, they were really not developing a new hermeneutic as such. But what we get from the Victorines was simply a preoccupation with the literal-historical sense apart from the allegorical or spiritualizing senses.

B. THE HIGH MIDDLE AGES

1. *The Place of the Bible in Theology.* Here it is important to think of the school, the university. This period becomes known as Scholasticism, because theology is connected to the schools. The schools are the newly founded universities. Theology and the study of Scripture undergo quite a shift here as they move from the monastery to the university classroom. We have pictured the monk living, praying, eating, and sleeping Scripture, living his life in the context of the life of Scripture, whereas in the school, not unlike our present situation, Scripture is a subject of academic study. What we get in the school approach is a distinction or separation between theology and exegesis, a distinction or separation between the discipline of theology and the discipline of biblical interpretation. This is in part because of the influence of Aristotelian philosophy away from Platonic philosophy. With

Aristotle, reality is seen contained in the thing itself. Hence in scriptural study, attention shifts to the sense of the letter. With the reality seen in the thing itself, rather than being mirrored into some other-worldly realm of the spiritual, Scripture itself becomes the object of study. What the Holy Spirit intended to say is there in Scripture, and all the levels of meaning are in the letter of the text, not in some other levels of meaning.

With a shift in scriptural study there is a shift in theology. While work on the Bible becomes more "literal" and "historical" (though, remember, we are still in the twelfth and thirteenth centuries), theology becomes speculative. An important influence on this shift in theology is the interest in dialectic (a part of logic). In the university situation, dialectic is the analysis of a question. Speculation is looking into something. It could and did have mystical overtones because theology first and foremost is looking into God. A question is posed, alternatives analyzed, often followed by a resolution. The shift in theology is a shift away from *sacra pagina* to *sacra doctrina* (sacred doctrine). The first question in Thomas' *Summa Theologiae* is: What is sacred doctrine? Work on the sacred page is contained in the *Commentaries* on Scripture. Theological questions are dealt with in the *Summaries* of theology (there were summaries in other disciplines as well). Theology then has a life of its own. Scripture and the Fathers are the authorities (footnotes). The method is philosophical, faith seeking understanding.

2. *The Interpretation of the Bible.* Accompanying the separation of Bible and theology is a different approach to the Bible (with Aristotle and reason in the background). For a Platonist, the soul (spirit) was seen hidden or imprisoned in the body (letter). The Aristotelian sees the spirit expressed by the text. All meaning is expressed in the letter, authored by God. The focus shifts away from the mirror of universal truths to the intention of the author (letter). To understand the author is to discern the words and

their significance. The Latin word to understand (*intelligere*) means to read within, to penetrate the rational meaning. The truth of the matter is there in the Bible expressed by the letters.

So far in Scholasticism we have the separation of biblical study from the study of theology, a different approach to theology (*sacra doctrina*), and a different approach to Scripture (intention of the letter). Also we have something of a new hermeneutic; at least a great deal is made of that in the scholarly literature. (One is always suspicious of new theories, because in the practice of biblical interpretation, the traditional results usually pertain.) This new theory is seen developed by the important fourteenth century Franciscan biblical scholar, Nicholas of Lyra, who in turn was the most important biblical commentator for the later Middle Ages and early Reformation. The new hermeneutic is called the "double literal sense." There are two senses or meanings expressed by the letter or word: the historical-literal sense, and the spiritual- or prophetic-literal sense. The example given is that Solomon may refer to Solomon the man, or be a figure of Christ, or both. If both, both were intended by the author, the Holy Spirit. As will be seen with Thomas, grounding everything in the letter does not preclude the use of the traditional fourfold sense (literal, allegorical, tropological, and anagogical). The theory of the double literal sense is widely accepted in the later Middle Ages (via Thomas and Nicholas). There will be an increasing attention to the text.

3. The key figure in the high Middle Ages is Thomas Aquinas. In the modern period Thomas is famous for his *Summa Theologiae* (Summary of Theology). In the century following his own, his commentaries on Scripture were more influential. Note that the Aristotelian Thomas wrote on Scripture, and in a separate literary genre he wrote on theology. As an Aristotelian thinks in terms of causality rather than reflection, Thomas thinks of God as the first author of Scripture and the human authors as instruments of divine revelation, choosing their own words. The letter

contains the intention of the inspired writer. Thomas outlined his approach to biblical interpretation in the following statement:

> The author of Holy Scripture is God, in whose power it is to signify his meaning, not by words only (as man also can do) but by things themselves. So, whereas in every other science things are signified by words, this science has the property that the things signified by the words have themselves also a signification. Therefore that first signification whereby words signify things belongs to the first sense, the historical or literal. That signification whereby things signified by words have themselves also a signification is called the spiritual sense, which is based on the literal, and presupposes it. For as the apostle says (Heb 10:1) the Old Law is a figure of the New Law, and (Pseudo-) Dionysius says: "The New Law itself is a figure of future glory." Again, in the New Law, whatever our Head had done is a type of what we ought to do. Therefore, so far as the things of the Old Law signify the things of the New Law, there is the allegorical sense; so far as the things done in Christ, or so far as the things which signify Christ are types of what we ought to do, there is the moral sense. But so far as they signify what relates to eternal glory, there is the anagogical sense. Since the literal sense is that which the author intends, and since the author of Holy Scripture is God, it is not unfitting, as Augustine says, if even according to the literal sense one word in Holy Scripture should have several senses (*Summa Theologiae* I.1.10).

Thomas presents a relationship between the Old and New Testaments along the lines of sign and fulfillment. The pattern is from Old to New to "future glory." Augustine is cited to show that in one literal sense there are several (spiritual) meanings. (It is always amazing how current Augustine is for the medievals on into the sixteenth century.) God is at work in the Old through types and signs of the New. In seeing the signs one sees the relationship between Old and New, and in seeing the spiritual sense of the New one sees the relationship between the New Testament and the church. In the allegorical, moral, and anagogical senses, God uses visible words to signify invisible truths. The pattern of relationship, fulfillment, and development from Old to New to church is the pattern of Thomas' theology, and his interpretation of Scripture fits within that organic pattern.

For Thomas, there is an organic unity between Old and New. Augustine's view of the progress of revelation is expanded by Thomas to include everything from beginning to end, from creation to history, through the history of Israel, Old and New, to the end of time. Thomas' view of revelation is that it is salvation history developing organically. God is working salvation in history, and so the history of God's people is salvation history. The history of salvation in Scripture is the development from Old to New, old law to evangelical law. The unity is based on God. The organic continuum goes on in the church to "eternal glory."

The main focus of Thomas on the Old and New Testament is on their organic development, a part of the larger focus of salvation history. In terms of Augustine's approach and categories, Thomas' approach is a blend of the providential and hermeneutical foci. The blend is seeing Testament as both era and book. Certain things concerning Christ are prefigured in the Old Testament through figures like David and Solomon. This is so because things of Christ are of such magnitude and power that they could not have been introduced "suddenly": "The things of Christ are so great that they would not have been believed unless they had first been disseminated gradually through the growth of time."[1] The development in time (era of salvation) is the development from imperfect to perfect. Also the Old Testament is a "figure" of the New Testament. The New Testament church is a "figure" of the glory of heaven. With the development of "figure," Old to New and New to glory, the Old Testament is a "figure of the figure." The development is the development of clarity. Thomas also refers the relationship of Old and New Laws to the relationship of seed to tree, implicit to explicit, fear to love. The growth is continual.

C. THE LATE MEDIEVAL PERIOD

1 and 2. *Scripture and Theology.* The fourteenth and fifteenth centuries are a mixture of what went before and some new currents of thought and practice. The schools continue to be the main focus of theological and biblical studies. There are currents of spirituality (for example, German mysticism and *Devotio moderna*) where the approach to Scripture is more along the monastic lines of *sacra pagina.* Among the Nominalists (a new philosophy-theology) and others, attention is paid to the relation of the Scriptures to the traditions of the church. Tension and even conflict between them is posited. The concentration on Scripture as an ancient book and the use of Scripture to criticize the church is intensified in the (very) late medieval movement of Humanism.

The fourfold method continues. The double-literal sense is used. The imitation of Christ is another emphasis. The use of Jewish resources for a more historical understanding of the Old Testament increases. Study of Hebrew and Greek grows tremendously. All of these interests and approaches are filtered into the Reformation through the Humanists. The most important work on Scripture at the beginning of the sixteenth century was done by the Humanists. In the Catholic Reformation the Humanists led the way for critical editions of Scripture, vernacular translations, and the study of the Greek and Latin classics (as opposed to the Scholastics). They were defeated at the mid-sixteenth century Council of Trent. It has been in our century that Catholics have adopted Humanist and modern critical approaches to Scripture. The Protestants generally welcomed and used Humanist scholarship.

The Humanists were involved in all kinds of humane studies. For our purposes let us peg their efforts around the printing press. So the approaches to Scripture in the medieval church differed as it was handled by the monks (*sacra pagina*), by the schoolmen (*sacra doctrina*), and by the printers (the book). That is an enormous development, the effects of which we are still appropriating: the relation of the Holy Book to the traditions of the church, to the study of theology, and to the life of faith.

The effect of the Humanists on the place and interpretation of Scripture in the church centered around their sense of history, study of the classics, expertise in the biblical (original) languages, preparation of critical printed editions of the Bible, and the use of Scripture for the reform of the church. (Note that their effect on the place and interpretation of Scripture is on the church in general, not just on theology, since their programs were broader than technical theology.)

A growing sense among the Renaissance thinkers (south of the Alps) and Humanists (north) is that the historical past is distant and different from present culture. This sense was not universally accepted, and it took about until the nineteenth century for historical consciousness to be widely accepted and then largely only in Western culture. Their sense of history was that the time and place of classical culture was in the ancient world— not their own. In general for the medievals the age of the Bible was their own, a timelessness to it all. The Humanist perspective was the separation of past from present.

The Humanists were scholars, students of antiquity. The general Renaissance of the time was a revival of the arts, literature, and learning. The Humanists were interested in the learning contained in classical literature. The study of the classics was to go along with the study of Scripture, which also was from the classical world, for the purpose of moral and intellectual reform of the church, theology, philosophy, education—the whole program. The critical study of the past had the edge to it of informing and often attacking the present. The study of the past included the editing, printing, and learning from the Church Fathers.

The Humanists were part and parcel of the revival of Hebrew and Greek studies. Study of the ancient world meant the recovery of their languages. Study of the original languages of Scripture raised questions about the Latin Bible. The study of the Bible in the original often led to a criticism of the way the Bible had been translated into Latin and interpreted. Study of ancient languages was not what we would call strictly an academic exercise. Ancient literature, classical and Christian, was presumed to have real value. The Humanists were often critical of Scholastics and others who concentrated only on the literal meaning of the text.

Humanist interest in original languages included an interest in original manuscripts and codices. With their historical perspective on the editing, translating, and transmission of texts, they were concerned to get as far back as possible to the original version of a writing. For scriptural study, this concern led to the discovery, collating, and printing of early Hebrew and Greek codices of the Bible. In 1516 Erasmus published a Greek New Testament, based on the most ancient codices he could find. The sixteenth century witnessed several critical editions of the Bible, printed by movable type. The new method in printing made possible the multiplication of both critical editions and vernacular translations.

The study of classics, the Bible, and Church Fathers was critical and scholarly. The purpose of it was to reform the present. The Humanists were among those who were disturbed about corruption, lack of education, and the generally sorry state of society. The church was often blamed for most of it, blamed for being too interested in money, politics, war, everything but the care of souls. The attacks were bitter and sarcastic. Theology (Scholasticism) was reproached for being interested only in syllogisms, and not the simple piety of Scripture. The goal of their work was the reform of church and society through education for the purpose of piety and knowledge.

3. The key figure among the Humanists was Erasmus of Rotterdam. Writing at the turn of the sixteenth century (died in 1536), Erasmus was very critical. He lambasted the superstitions of current monastic practice, the ritualism and legalism connected with the Mass, Scholastic theology (especially its preoccupation with propositions, corollaries, definitions, and conclusions), the worldliness of the Pope (especially his preoccupation with war, money, excommunications, and interdicts), the begging of mendicant friars, clerical concubinage, and so on. The basis of his attacks was a call to return to the source of Scripture in its purity and original meaning for Christian living. The "pagan" classics and Church Fathers were to serve as an orientation to Scripture.

Erasmus edited and published a number of the works of the Fathers. Against criticism, he continued to advocate the study of the classics: "A sensible reading of the pagan poets and philosophers is a good preparation for the Christian life." He distinguished between the bad morals of the pagans, which are not to be followed, and their many examples of right living. "To break in on" Scripture without the preparation of the classics is almost sacrilegious: "St. Cyprian has worked wonders in adorning the Scriptures with the literary beauty of the ancients."[2] So guided by the Fathers of the early church, classical studies were taken as a necessary prolegomenon to understanding Christian revelation.

Schooled by the Brethren of the Common Life (a part of late medieval *Devotio moderna*), Erasmus' orientation to theology was away from speculation toward piety. His orientation to Scripture, the source of Christian piety, was toward the example of Jesus. The ethical life, preaching, and teaching of Jesus combine into the philosophy of Christ, the source of reform for everything from the papacy to peasantry.

Erasmus' main interest and work was the New Testament. His Greek New Testament with critical annotations was a milestone in Reformation work on the Bible. It was used by Luther immediately. Erasmus could be very critical of the people of the Old Testament, for their superstitious and barbarous ways, in comparison with the "good letters" from Greece and Rome. In medieval terms, his approach to the New Testament was largely tropological—as in Christ, so in me.

Erasmus' sarcasm against Scholastic theology included his charge of supercilious speculation, especially the use of dialectic. Theology was too intellectually preoccupied with doctrine, and not with its main task—persuading and bringing people to the way of Christ. Practical piety is the point of it all. When contemporary commentators dealt with the New Testament, Erasmus complained that they concentrated only on the literal sense:

> Let me mention another requirement for a better understanding of Holy Scripture [the first being, reading Scripture with a clean heart]. I would suggest that you read those commentators who do not stick so closely to the literal sense. The ones I would recommend most highly after St. Paul himself are Origen, Ambrose, Jerome, and Augustine. Too many of our modern theologians are prone to a literal interpretation, which they subtly misconstrue. They do not delve into the mysteries, and they act as if St. Paul were not speaking the truth when he says that our law is spiritual. There are some of these theologians who are so completely taken up with these human commentators that they relegate what the Fathers had to say to the realm of dreams. They are so

entranced with the writings of Duns Scotus that, without ever having read the Scriptures, they believe themselves to be competent theologians. I care not how subtle their distinctions are; they are certainly not the final word on what pertains to the Holy Spirit.[3]

In their theology the Scholastics were too speculative; in their commentaries on Scripture they were too literal. So a leading scholar of the Renaissance calls for a pious reading of the Bible as the source for Christian living.

D. THE EARLY REFORMATION

1. *The Place of the Bible in Theology.* The early Reformers, for example, Luther, Zwingli, and Calvin, were very concerned about the place of the Bible in everything—church, theology, and especially preaching. The main point of the Reformation was that the gospel must be proclaimed. To keep our schematization going, think pulpit, think of the Evangelical cities (Wittenberg, Zurich, Geneva) where the medium for information was the pulpit (along with the important pamphlets). The Reformation was a movement of the Word: Christ, preaching, Scripture—in that order. They all are the Word of God. The Reformers used the printed Word, studied the Word, prayed the Word. But their concern was to bring preaching back into the Mass, preaching in the vernacular, and preaching on the text of Scripture. When Luther said that the church is not a pen-house but a mouth-house, he meant that the good news cannot properly be put in (dead) letters but is to be proclaimed loudly (in German).

What the Scholastics separated—theology and commentary on Scripture—the early Reformers sought to bring together again, along the lines of *sacra pagina* (minus the monastery). Scripture alone is the sole authority for the church, the discipline of theology, and the life of faith. The Reformers continued the call for the reform of the church on the basis of Scripture. Every office and activity in the church falls under the judgment of Scripture. All of theology is contained in Scripture. God has revealed all that we need to know about him in Christ. Calvin is especially strong on the knowledge of God, the beginning point of his *Institutes of the Christian Religion.* God is revealed in Scripture, and to see the revelation of God in nature we need the spectacles of Scripture. Theology must be biblical theology, for any other kind is human invention.

Scripture is its own authority because it is clear. No other authority is needed to see through its meaning. The early Reformers were not concerned about some theory of inspiration. That came later. The Bible is the Word. The Reformers were aware of the "critical" discussions among the Humanists about the text, authorship, language, etc. Luther engaged in some of this. The point of the Word is its/his is-ness, the presence of the Word in Scripture-church-preaching. The Humanist sense of the distance of Scripture from the present was not accepted. The Scholastic separation of theology from Scripture was attacked. The purpose of theology is to serve preaching, the main task of the church. The vast amount of theological literature from the early Reformation was intended to clear the roadblocks to Scripture and to facilitate the proclamation of that gospel.

2. *The Interpretation of the Bible.* The early Reformers were pre-modern; they continued the general medieval understanding of interpretation as commentary, annotation, and exposition. The modern interpreter continues to develop the Humanist perspective of the historical past; thus interpretation in modern time is bridging the gulf between ancient literature and modern thinking. The early Reformers continued the monkish approach of total immersion into the thinking and language of Scripture so that there is only one language, one biblical theology.

In their Catholic context, the Reformers emphasized that Scripture was its own interpreter. Luther argued that the papacy had built a wall of authoritative interpretation around itself so that Scripture could only be read as the papacy interpreted it. One late medieval synthesis had it that Scripture is to tradition as foundation is to interpretation (Occam). Strong in the sixteenth century was the question of an authoritative interpretation of Scripture. The Catholic Council of Trent decreed

> that no one, relying on his own skill, in matters of faith, and of morals pertaining to the edification of Christian doctrine, wresting the Sacred Scriptures to his own senses, presume to interpret the said Sacred Scripture contrary to that sense which holy mother church, whose it is to judge of the true sense and interpretation of the Holy Scripture, has held and does hold.[4]

For Calvin at this time, the interpretation of Scripture by Scripture alone is aided by the internal testimony of the Holy Spirit. Scripture itself attests to its message and meaning. Christ and the Spirit are at work in the Word. The Reformers insisted that post-apostolic claims of authoritative interpretation were precisely the reason why the Word of God lost its/his central place in the life of the church.

The Reformation interpretation of Scripture was caught up in polemics. The Humanists used Scripture to attack the church, but they were not so much interested in the pure doctrines of Scripture as they were in exposing the corruption and folly of the present situation in the light of the piety of Scripture. The early Reformers fought it out theologically on the basis of Scripture (and the Fathers). The doctrine of justification by faith alone, by grace alone (by Christ alone), was seen as the central doctrine of Scripture. The doctrine of justification by faith is the criterion by which all other doctrines, offices, and practices in the church are judged. The criteriological priority of justification by faith is established in Scripture. The church stands or falls, said Luther, on the scriptural teaching of justification. There were other issues, other polemics, but the procedure was the same. Doctrinal reform was forged and pleaded on the basis of Scripture.

3. In the early Reformation period Martin Luther was the key figure. Basic for Luther's understanding of Scripture was his distinction between law and gospel. The gospel of Jesus Christ is the fulfillment and end of the Mosaic law. Law and gospel are in all books of the Bible. The gospel is the good news that salvation is in Christ alone. Abraham and others saw that gospel in the promises, believed, and were justified. Luther transposes Augustine's distinction between Old Testament and New Testament as ways of salvation to law and gospel as ways of salvation. The way of the law is do this . . . and don't do that. . . . The way of the gospel is believe . . . and it has already been done for you (in Christ). The law is command, the gospel is gift, the gift of forgiveness. When the law commands, failure results because one cannot fulfill the law on one's own power ("The good I would, I do not"). The law humbles; the gospel picks up. One cannot be picked up unless one is put down to size. Being brought low (law) and being raised up (gospel) are the ups and downs of the Christian life, the experience of sin (brought by the law) and the experience of forgiveness (brought by Christ). The distinction between law and gospel, the doctrine of justification by faith apart from works, and the understanding of the core of Scripture are all the same for Luther.

The center of Scripture for Luther is Christ, present in both the Old Testament and the New Testament. Christ is the eternal Word of God, present in Old Testament times in the form of promise, present in New Testament times in the person of Jesus, and present in the church through word and sacrament. In all cases, Christ the Word is the effective means of grace (healing salvation for Augustine). The center or core of Scripture is "what drives Christ" (*was Christum treibet*) (impossible to translate literally), i.e., what preaches Christ, what promotes or points to

Christ. Christ is at the core of God's plan of salvation. God promises through prophets; God delivers in person. All of Scripture leads to Christ, and Christ leads to salvation.

Luther's response to the various senses of meaning in the Middle Ages (fourfold, double-literal) was that Scripture has one simple sense (most often, Christ). Or Luther will talk about the grammatical sense as the meaning of the text, that the grammatical meaning and theological meaning are the same. Luther availed himself of Humanist scholarship (and Humanists saw an early ally in Luther) and was a part of a late medieval trend to highlight (once again) the christological meaning of a text. Luther also used allegory, not to establish a doctrine, he said, but to embellish it. He also used the other spiritual senses. Luther on Scripture is often presented as a total break from the medieval world. That came later. (You can take the boy out of the monastery, but you cannot take the monastery out of the boy.) In the area of the senses of meaning, Luther is a part of the medieval trend to call for a return to the letter of the text, and then, in practice, to go on and find other senses of meaning. After all (and all the medievals knew this) the New Testament itself uses allegory.

Luther's distinction is his construction of Scripture as containing a single testament (will, promise) of Christ. God's last and only will and testament is that he would die for our salvation. The promise is the declaration of the will and testament. The death of the God-Man validates his testament. The inheritance is the forgiveness of sins and eternal life. The (new) testament of Christ is eternal. It is played out in time, but there is no development in the eternal. Augustine and the medievals generally saw a development and transformation within and between the Old and New Testaments. Luther held that the New Testament is older than the Old because it is the oldest (eternal). The Old Testament begins and ends in time.

We have come a long way (to the sixteenth century). Or have

we? What often is seen to be new is not so new after all. The monastery (*sacra pagina*), the university (*sacra doctrina*), the printing press (holy book), and the pulpit (holy gospel) represent shifts and emphases. But the whole thing was still "sacred."

PART TWO: THE EARLY MODERN CHURCH

In the modern period the historical-critical method dominates most Protestant approaches to Scripture and, since 1943 (*Divino Afflante Spiritu*), also most Catholic approaches. By the middle of the eighteenth century the historical-critical method is in place. One way of picturing the shift that takes place between the medieval approach (including early Reformation) and the modern approach of the later seventeenth and eighteenth century is to consider their views of the relation between the letter and the real, between the text of Scripture and what really happened. In the medieval approach the letter of the Bible was read as historical and real; there was no question that what was said really happened. Scripture was read as religion, history, geography, liturgy, prayer, and so on. The approach of historical criticism is first to question the relation between the letter and the real, then to posit a separation between the two, and finally to see the text as a faith response to a real stimulus. What we have in the text are the responses of the communities of faith, not the stimuli. In the nineteenth century it was said that what we have in the New Testament is the Christ of faith and not the Jesus of history. In any case, it came to be perceived in historical criticism that the Bible is the interpretation of facts and not the bare facts themselves. It was written from faith to (our) faith.

The historical-critical method is concerned about the origin of individual books of the Bible. Concerned about the books as theological literature and not history, it uses the best critical (objective, analytic) tools available for the study of ancient literature. The modern approach develops some of the humanist interests detailed earlier—interest in the historical past, the original text, and language.

There were and are various methods within the historical-critical method. These will be detailed by others in this volume. Here the concern will be to trace the rise of the historical-critical method, to detail the shift from medieval-early Reformation to early modern approaches (from the middle of the sixteenth century to late eighteenth century). Generally the medievals treated Scripture as the Church's holy book. The moderns increasingly treat Scripture with secular tools of historical and literary criticism in order to understand it better in its ancient setting.

Among the elements that contributed to the rise of the historical-critical method include the following: methodology (discussion of the way of interpretation), Deism (rational belief in the deity, with resultant rationalism and the disciplines of biblical introduction and biblical theology), textual criticism (analysis of codices, variant readings, with both theory and practice), and historical consciousness (awareness of distance and difference, e.g., seeing the difference between stimulus and response).

1. Theology became interested in the questions of "method" in the sixteenth century.[5] In 1555 Nils Hemmingsen, a student of Luther and Melanchthon (especially the latter), published a book *On Methods,* the first part for philosophy, the second for theological method. It was important because of its subject—*methodus.* Earlier in the sixteenth century method as a technical term came into medicine, and in the second half of the century lawyers discussed method. So theology joined the other branches of learning in their concern to tidy up their discipline. Also important is that Hemmingsen brought logic (particularly dialectic) into theology in the discussion of method. For biblical study this meant that discussion of "exegetical method" (the way to interpret) was carried on in the part on philosophical method, and then practiced in theology and "exegesis," the actual word being used.

"Exegesis" is widely used in the seventeenth and eighteenth

whom is it written? What was its place in the community? When was it written and in what language? What questions are there about the Greek translation? Who wrote it? What about the literary technique? Is it canonical? What is its content? In this line-up there are ten questions raised before the question of content, because the message is linked to its historical place.

The discipline of introduction presupposes the relativity of each book. Each book is unique unto itself and demands a thorough, objective (= critical) study in order to understand it. Later in the eighteenth century, John Eichhorn developed further the humanist-rationalist introduction (three volumes on the Old Testament, 1780–83). The Old Testament must be studied like any other literature, free from all authorities, dogma, and tradition.

The discipline of biblical theology follows closely on the discipline of biblical introduction. The discipline of biblical theology, seen by some as the crown of biblical scholarship, comes out of the Enlightenment and the critical methodologies we have been detailing. More particularly, Gotthold Lessing's *Education of Mankind* (1780) constructed a view of the Bible which parochialized it as preparatory to the maturation of the human race. The Old Testament came at the stage of the childhood of the race, which was motivated by temporal rewards and punishments (law). The New Testament fits into the adolescence of the race, where one is willing to put up with temporary hardships with the promise of greater (spiritual) rewards later (resurrection). And finally the race matured by the Enlightenment, where one lives in the here and now guided by reason alone. In effect, then, the Bible is put in its time and place.

Later in the eighteenth century the concern was to separate biblical theology from dogmatic theology (1758, *The Advantage of Biblical Theology over Scholasticism;* 1787, *The Difference between Biblical Theology and Dogmatic Theology*). Dogmatic theology, perhaps connected to philosophy, could have permanence, while biblical theology is connected to its history. Late eighteenth century Romanticism, with its emphasis on empathy, aided the discipline of biblical theology. Something like today's nostalgia, one could emotionally immerse oneself into the spirit of a past generation. Biblical theology is the theology of a book. If a book has a human situation—authorship, time, audience, language, purpose, content, method—then it also has a particular theology. As there are various books with various historical situations, so there are various books with various theologies. As a result of this eighteenth century development, there is no such thing as biblical theology in the singular, only biblical theologies (plural).

3. Erasmus' text of the Greek New Testament, the first published in 1516, as mentioned earlier, remained the "critical" edition (*textus receptus*) until well into the nineteenth century. Although the Complutensian Polyglot relied on earlier manuscript evidence, and was actually printed earlier (*New Testament*, 1514) though made public in 1522, and is now regarded as better, it was Erasmus' text, through subsequent editions, that was "received by all" (*textus receptus*) and seemed to have an over three hundred year right to be. Robert Stephanus' text (Paris, 1550), which followed Erasmus (1535 edition), became the *textus receptus* for Britain. The edition of the printing firm, Elzevir (Leiden, 1633), which followed Stephanus, became the *textus receptus* for the Continent. Richard Simon, later in the seventeenth century, engaged in a critical investigation into textual variants. In 1734 Johann Bengel (Tübingen) issued a critical text, not exactly the *textus receptus,* and is regarded as important for modern scientific textual criticism, because of his principles (e.g., the more difficult reading is preferred) and theories of manuscript families (groupings of manuscripts). Johann Wettstein's Greek New Testament (1751–52, Amsterdam) contained many important (new) variants. Johannes Griesbach (text, 1774–75) agreed with Bengel on the grouping of manuscript families. His theories have lived on in textual criticism (e.g., a reading must have an ancient witness, the shorter as well as the more difficult is preferred).

And so on went the reception of the *textus receptus* until 1831, when Karl Lachmann set it aside and published a text based entirely on ancient manuscripts. (In 1881, Westcott and Hort published *The New Testament in the Original Greek,* which has become in effect a new *textus receptus.*)

Textual criticism, with the thousands and thousands of manuscripts and the tens of thousands of variant readings, was complicated not only by the discipline itself but also by the tradition (church) that has received the biblical text. Critical interpretation of the text developed earlier under the aegis of rationalism. Critical rendering of the text itself was slower to develop not only because Erasmus' text was based on late evidence but also because it has seldom been regarded as purely a scientific task.

4. What developed in Humanism, a sense of historical distance from the past, including Scripture, continued to develop in the early modern period with all the critical methodologies.

Historical consciousness, or the dawning thereof, is part and parcel of what we have been discussing. The problem of hermeneutics as the problem of understanding and language is brought into the nineteenth century by Friedrich Schleiermacher, and beyond our scope. Hermeneutics as the problem of expression, interpretation and translation is brought into focus in the early modern period with the rise of the historical-critical method. Key in this development is the separation between text and reader, namely the consciousness of the separation.

One way of describing this development is the distinction between internalization and externalization used in the sociology of knowledge. In the medieval-early Reformation periods, as our argument has gone, the reader internalized Scripture, morning, noon, and night. With Humanism—printing, editing, translating, introducing—developed the externalization of the Bible as an ancient text. The concern of methodology is to find the way(s) of bridging the gap between text and interpreter. Once interpretation (with historical consciousness) becomes the focus of biblical study, then the Orthodox needed to set up a system, with logical coherence, to make the Lutheran interpretation the correct one vis-à-vis the Roman and the Reformed traditions. The emancipator from Orthodox dogmatism is always described as reason (and on to Rationalism). But Orthodoxy used philosophy, and Pietism contributed another crucial element in the emancipation—the subjective experience of the individual. So this perspective suggests that orthodox philosophy plus pietist individualism helped create the atmosphere for Rationalism, where the externalization process is advanced. The Bible is to be treated as any other ancient document, in need of historical introduction and linguistic-literary analysis. The distance and task is enormous.

Biblical theology belongs to the ancient world. Dogmatic theology, conscious of its methodology and distance from Scripture, is part of the church's tradition, also past. If there is to be a bridge between biblical theology and contemporary thinking, it is the task of hermeneutics (translation, interpretation, understanding) to bridge the gulf—and on to the problems of the nineteenth century.

It is with historical consciousness that problems are perceived that were not before—method, exegesis, critical text, interpretation, and hermeneutics—all with the positive use of reason. The rise of the historical-critical method itself is an historical phenomenon. Its posture today is that it is purely objective and scientific. It did not begin that way nor develop untouched by human historical elements. Practitioners of the historical-critical method may want to use the method on itself and see it in its historical setting, which this essay has tried to set out with pure objectivity. The usual survey of the historical-critical method is described with "advance" language, not totally absent from the foregoing. As one author put it, going through the centuries, "It finally won out!" What did it win, outside of control of academic biblical studies? Did it win any new or better or clearer understanding of the text that was unavailable to St. Augustine, Thomas, Luther, or Calvin?

NOTES

1. Cited in K. Hagen, *A Theology of Testament in the Young Luther* (Leiden: Brill, 1974) 47.

2. *Enchiridion* (1503) cited in *The Essential Erasmus,* J.P. Dolan, ed. (New York: New American Library, 1964) 36.

3. *Ibid.,* 37.

4. P. Schaff, *The Creeds of Christendom,* Vol. 2 (New York: Harper, 1919) 83.

5. K. Hagen, " 'De exegetica methodo,' Nils Hemmingsen's *De Methodis* (1555)," Duke Monographs in Medieval and Renaissance Studies, in press.

RECOMMENDED READINGS

John W. Aldridge, *The Hermeneutic of Erasmus* (Richmond: John Knox, 1966). Basic level; concentrates on the philosophy of Christ, erudition, and philology.

Cambridge History of the Bible, three volumes (Cambridge: Cambridge University Press, 1963–70). Reference volumes by specialists that cover the early period (I), medieval (II), and modern (III).

Robert Grant, *A Short History of the Interpretation of the Bible* (New York: Macmillan, 1948/63). Basic introduction that starts with the Bible itself.

Herbert F. Hahn, *The Old Testament in Modern Research* (Philadelphia: Fortress, 1954/66). Extensive survey of Old Testament criticism; strong on the moderns.

Willen J. Kooiman, *Luther and the Bible,* tr. John Schmidt (Philadelphia: Muhlenberg, 1961). Introductory level, aimed at a broad coverage of many facets.

Werner Kümmel, *The New Testament: The History of the Investigation of Its Problems,* tr. S.M. Gilmour and H.C. Kee (Nashville: Abingdon, 1972). Extensive survey of New Testament criticism; several primary sources. Emphasis on the moderns.

Henri de Lubac, *The Sources of Revelation,* tr. L. O'Neill (New York: Herder and Herder, 1968). An abridgement of his monumental work in French on patristic and medieval exegesis; emphasis on the spiritual understanding of Scripture.

Beryl Smalley, *The Study of the Bible in the Middle Ages* (Oxford: Blackwell, 1952). Scholarly and readable history from the Fathers of the Church to the friars of the thirteenth century.

Peter Stuhlmacher, *Historical Criticism and Theological Interpretation of Scripture,* tr. R. Harrisville (Philadelphia: Fortress, 1977). Short overview from the ancients to the twentieth century; reconstruction of the current dilemma.

Daniel J. Harrington, S.J.

Catholic Interpretation of Scripture

THE BIBLE IN CATHOLIC LIFE TODAY

A friend who by upbringing and conviction is an evangelical Christian made a comment some time ago that startled me. He said that whenever he has had occasion to attend Roman Catholic liturgies recently, he has been struck by how "Protestant" they sounded. He meant that as a compliment, and he went on to explain that what makes him feel at home in Catholic worship today is the massive dose of biblical language—not only in the readings taken directly from the Scriptures but also in the songs and the prayers. His comment led me, as a professional biblical scholar who also preaches and presides regularly at worship services in the Catholic church, to reflect on a dramatic development in my own church.

The foundations for this development were already laid in the 1940s and 1950s by Pope Pius XII's encyclical on biblical studies (*Divino Afflante Spiritu*) and his revision of the liturgical services for Holy Week. But the decisive turning point was the Second Vatican Council. Building upon the directives approved by Pope Pius XII and worked out in more detail by biblical scholars and theologians, the council fathers affirmed in a powerful way the importance of the Bible in the life of the Catholic church.

Before we look at the key document relating to the Bible from Vatican II, it may be useful to contrast the place of the Bible in the Catholic church before the council and its place today. The three areas for contrast are liturgy, theological education, and ecumenism.

Prior to Vatican II, Scripture was certainly an integral part of the Mass. A selection from a New Testament epistle or the Old Testament, as well as a passage from one of the gospels, was read at every eucharistic service. The priest read these biblical selections in Latin, while some of the laity followed along with the help of an English translation. On Sundays, the passages were also read aloud in English, either as an accompaniment to the Latin or after it. The range of Scripture readings was narrow and repetitive. Matthew's gospel with its emphases on church order and Petrine authority was especially prominent.

Vatican II removed the language barrier by decreeing that the sacred liturgy could now be celebrated in modern languages as well as Latin. The Bible is now read in English (or whatever language is most appropriate), and the readings have a very prominent place. Shortly after the council, the liturgists worked out a new and more comprehensive cycle of Scripture readings. For Sundays there is a three-year cycle, each Sunday having passages from the Old Testament, the Book of Psalms, the New Testament epistles, and the gospels. For weekdays there is a two-year cycle consisting of a passage from the Old Testament or the New Testament epistles, a psalm, and the gospels. This development means that in their worship services, Catholics today are exposed to large amounts of Scripture in the language that they most readily understand.

Prior to Vatican II, the Bible was not ordinarily read directly as part of the primary or secondary school program in religious education. In Catholic colleges, the study of the Bible was supplemented by conservative textbooks that guided students along approved paths. In the training of Catholic priests, biblical courses were usually placed at the end of the program, after the proper dogmatic theological foundations were already in place. Professors of Scripture in pre-Vatican II seminaries were generally very cautious not to stray into the realms of dogmatic theology or moral theology. They focused on philological and historical matters. What they taught were officially classified as "minor courses."

Vatican II made clear that biblical studies are central in Catholic theology. In the many years that I have taught in Catholic seminaries since 1971, I have never heard a student question or complain about the need for Scripture courses. These courses are taken at the beginning, middle, and end of seminary programs. The students work hard at these courses and enjoy them. The professors dialogue with and even teach courses with their colleagues in systematic and moral theology. At every level in the Catholic educational system—colleges, high schools, grammar schools, religious education classes—the Bible is read and discussed. Catholics are becoming increasingly familiar with the language and themes of Scripture, and thus better able to appreciate their language of worship.

My Protestant friend's comment about the more "biblical" character of Catholic life raises the issue about the ecumenical significance of the Bible for Catholics. Prior to Vatican II, many Catholics looked upon the Bible as a "Protestant" book. Those Catholics who read it were careful to follow officially approved handbooks and commentaries, and loyally defended the need for such authoritative guidance from the teaching offices of the church. Those who quoted the Bible except to affirm traditional theological positions were considered peculiar or even dangerous.

Vatican II has encouraged Catholics to claim the Bible as

their own book. On local, national, and international levels, the Bible has emerged as the common ground for Catholics and Protestants. Both groups have become sensitive to their shared heritage in Scripture and have recognized that many of their sharpest differences come from post-biblical developments. These differences are real and touch on genuine issues, but must not obscure what Catholics and Protestants hold in common.

Within Catholic circles there is great enthusiasm for courses and lectures on the Bible. Books about the Bible and translations of the Bible are big sellers. A whole industry of lectures on the Bible that are available in the form of cassettes has sprung up. All these developments show that Catholics now look upon the Bible as "their" book too, see it as a means toward Christian unity, and want to know as much about it as they can.

A very concrete instance of the ecumenical possibility and power of the Bible is the fact that when the new Catholic lectionary was prepared in response to Vatican II, it was adopted (with minor modifications) by several mainline Protestant churches—Lutheran, Episcopal, Methodist, and Presbyterian. This means that on almost every Sunday the same set of Scripture readings is read and preached upon in all these Christian communities. The historical and theological differences between these groups remain, but at least they are dealing with the same basic texts of the Bible.

VATICAN II's CONSTITUTION
ON DIVINE REVELATION

The most compact and authoritative statement on the theory and theology of the Bible's place in the Catholic church is Vatican II's Constitution on Divine Revelation (known also by its Latin title *Dei Verbum*).[1] That document was issued in November 1965, but the way had been prepared for it by Pope Pius XII's 1943 encyclical *Divino Afflante Spiritu* and by several other official statements through the years. The conciliar document summarized the important points in those earlier statements and pushed Catholic biblical study out of some old ruts and onto better paths.

The first chapter of the six chapters in the Constitution deals with "divine revelation itself." Before the council and even in the early stages of the drafting of the document, there had been a lively debate about the nature of divine revelation, with many theologians (in the wake of Vatican I's insistence on the content of faith) stressing the primacy of the theological propositions revealed in the Bible. Without denying the content of revelation and its propositional dimension, the final draft of the council's Constitution stresses the primacy of God's revelation of himself as a person in relationship to his people. The personal dimension of revelation makes possible the propositional dimension: "By divine revelation God wished to manifest and communicate both himself and the eternal decrees of his will concerning the salvation of mankind" (§6). Both dimensions are clearly affirmed, but the personal aspect of revelation is given first place.

The second chapter, which concerns the transmission of divine revelation, takes up the problem of the relation between Scripture and tradition. Rejecting the idea that Scripture and tradition constitute two distinct sources of revelation, the Constitution insisted that they flow from "the same divine well-spring" (§9). It went on to state that "sacred tradition and Sacred Scripture make up a single sacred deposit of the Word of God, which is entrusted to the church" (§10). This emphasis on the unity of Scripture and tradition does not simply absorb the latter into the former: "The church does not draw her certainty about all revealed truths from the holy Scriptures alone" (§9). And the task of "giving an authentic interpretation" of both Scripture and tradition is entrusted to "the living teaching office of the church alone" (§10), though it is clearly stated that the ecclesiastical magisterium is "not superior to the Word of God, but is its servant" (§10). Thus the Constitution presents Scripture and tradition as one source of divine revelation while affirming the existence of tradition and making the ecclesiastical magisterium (the Pope and the bishops) the ultimate arbiter.

The third chapter is devoted to divine inspiration and its interpretation. The fact of inspiration is stated at the outset: "The divinely revealed realities, which are contained and presented in the text of Sacred Scripture, have been written down under the inspiration of the Holy Spirit" (§11). The same section presents a doctrine of the inerrancy of Scripture: "The books of Scripture, firmly, faithfully, and without error, teach that truth which God, for the sake of our salvation, wished to see confided to the sacred Scriptures." This may sound like a statement of limited inerrancy—that is, only what pertains to our salvation, and not historical or scientific matters, in the Bible is free from error. But, in fact, the theologians who wrote this document and the council fathers who voted their approval deliberately sought to avoid approving either complete inerrancy or limited inerrancy as the church's teaching. Since the Constitution was not a theological treatise and since the council fathers did not want to absolutize or give official sanction to one theologian or one school, there is no attempt to explain in detail *how* inspiration and inerrancy function or what scope these terms might have.[2] It was more a matter of reaffirming venerable theological teachings without specifying which interpretation of them is best.

The section on the interpretation of Scripture (§12) is the most important part for biblical scholars. Taking its cue from *Divino Afflante Spiritu,* the Constitution urged biblical scholars and indeed all Catholics (1) to pay attention to the literary forms in which divine revelation is expressed, (2) to look to the meaning that the biblical author intended in his own historical situation and culture, and (3) to consider the customary and characteristic patterns of perception, speech, and narrative prevailing at that time. Since this part of the document summarizes so well the tasks undertaken by Catholic biblical scholars, it deserves to be quoted in full:

> In determining the intention of the sacred writers, attention must be paid, *inter alia,* to "literary forms, for the fact is that truth is differently presented and expressed in the various types of historical writing, in prophetical and poetical texts," and in other forms of literary expression. Hence the exegete must look for that meaning which the sacred writer, in a determined situation and given the circumstances of his time and culture, intended to express and did in fact express, through the medium of a contemporary literary form. Rightly to understand what the sacred author wanted to affirm in his work, due attention must be paid both to the customary and characteristic patterns of perception, speech and narrative which prevailed at the age of the sacred writer, and to the conventions which the people of his time followed in their dealings with one another.

The freedom of research expressed in this paragraph is somewhat tempered by a reminder that biblical interpretation is "ultimately subject to the judgment of the church which exercises the divinely conferred commission and ministry of watching over and interpreting the word of God" (§12). The connection between the doctrine of the divine inspiration of Scripture and the task of interpreting Scripture in its historical context is drawn by using the formula "the words of God, expressed in the words of men" (§13).

In the fourth chapter, the Constitution defends the divinely inspired character and lasting value of the Old Testament (§14). It does so by alluding to some of the ways in which the Old Testament has been viewed in Christian theology: preparation for and prophecy of the coming of Christ, a source for understanding God and his dealings with his people, and a storehouse of sublime teaching on God and of sound wisdom on human life (§15). It also mentions that the books of the Old Testament contain "matters imperfect and provisional," without specifying what these are (cultic rules, calls for vengeance, ethically questionable actions?) and what Catholics are to do with them. Again it is important to remember that the Constitution is not a theology textbook but rather a statement of directions agreed upon and approved by the Catholic bishops of the world.

The chapter on the New Testament strikes a cautious balance between recognition of the complex process by which the four gospels came into being and affirmation of the basic truth of their portraits of Jesus:

> Holy Mother Church has firmly and with absolute constancy maintained and continues to maintain, that the four gospels just named, whose historicity she unhesitatingly affirms, faithfully hand on what Jesus, the Son of God, while he lived among men, really did and taught for their eternal salvation, until the day when he was taken up (see Acts 1:1–2). For, after the ascension of the Lord, the apostles handed on to their hearers what he had said and done, but with that fuller understanding which they, instructed by the glorious events of Christ and enlightened by the Spirit of truth, now enjoyed. The sacred authors, in writing the four gospels, selected certain of the many elements which had been handed on, either orally or already in written form, others they synthesized or explained with an eye to the situation of the churches, the while sustaining the form of preaching, but always in such a fashion that they have told us the honest truth about Jesus. Whether they relied on their own memory and recollections or on the testimony

of those who "from the beginning were eyewitnesses
and ministers of the Word," their purpose in writing
was that we might know the "truth" concerning the
things of which we have been informed (see Lk 1:2–4).

This statement in section §19 leaves room and indeed encourages
biblical scholars to do research on the literary forms, sources, and
final editing of the gospels. But it demands that they not lose
sight of the historical person of Jesus of Nazareth—the one to
whom the gospels bear witness.[3] The Pauline epistles and the
New Testament writings are said to formulate more precisely the
authentic teaching of Christ, preach the saving power of his divine work, and foretell its glorious consummation (§20).

The sixth chapter, which deals with Sacred Scripture in the
life of the church, provides the directions that have brought
about the biblical renewal of recent years. The opening statement
in §21 stresses the link between the Scriptures and the eucharistic
body of Christ. Far from separating the two, the Constitution
speaks of "the one table of the word of God and the body of
Christ." It insists that "all the preaching of the church . . . should
be nourished and ruled by Sacred Scripture" (§21), that access to
Scripture "ought to be wide open to the Christian faithful" (§22),
and that study of the "sacred page should be the very soul of sacred theology" (§24). Thus the post-Vatican II developments
with respect to the Bible's place in the life of the church are best
seen as faithful responses to the spirit of the council, not as de-
viations from it or as a new movement apart from it. If any doubt
remained about the central role of biblical studies in the seminary
curriculum and the piety of the church's ministers, the next-to-
last section of the Constitution speaks very clearly: "All clerics,
particularly priests of Christ and others who, as deacons or ca-
techists, are officially engaged in the ministry of the Word,
should immerse themselves in the Scriptures by constant sacred
reading and diligent study" (§25).

Vatican II's Constitution on Divine Revelation has given important and fruitful directions to the biblical movement in the Catholic church. The most significant directions are summarized by the following list: the emphasis on God's personal revelation as the basis for whatever propositional revelation may be contained in Scripture, the insistence that Scripture and tradition flow from "the same divine well-spring," the forthright acceptance of the historical and literary study of the Scriptures, the respect for the Old Testament, the cautious balance between the complexity of our gospels and their essential truth about Jesus, and the encouragement for Bible reading and study in every phase of the church's life.

There is much on this list with which evangelical and Lutheran Christians can agree, though their emphases may be slightly different. But some evangelicals might take exception to what might appear to be a doctrine of limited inerrancy expressed in the Constitution: "that truth which God, for the sake of our salvation, wished to see confided to the Sacred Scriptures" (§11). Both evangelicals and Lutherans will no doubt take strong exception to the idea of the ecclesiastical magisterium as the final arbiter of biblical interpretation (§§10, 12). They may also be skeptical about how well Catholics can manage to keep together Scripture and tradition on the one hand, and word and sacrament on the other hand. But however valid their objections may be, Protestants who take the trouble to read Vatican's II's Constitution on Divine Revelation cannot fail to recognize the "biblical" character of much of the language used in the document and the many direct references to Scripture throughout it. The council fathers opted for the language of the Bible rather than for the language of Scholastic theology.

THE WAYS OF CURRENT BIBLICAL SCHOLARSHIP

Up to this point we have considered the practical impact of biblical study on church life and an official statement about the place of the Bible in the church. Now is the time to focus on the methods used by Catholic biblical scholars—that is, what those men and women who devote themselves to research on the Scriptures do when they confront the biblical text.[4]

"Catholic biblical research" is obviously research done by Catholic scholars. Until recently, most biblical professionals were also ordained priests who taught in seminaries or on one of the international biblical faculties in Rome (Pontifical Biblical Institute) or Jerusalem (Ecole Biblique, Studium Biblicum Franciscanum). Since Vatican II, an increasing number of Catholic laymen and laywomen (as well as women religious) have obtained doctoral degrees in biblical studies and are now teaching at Catholic (and other) universities and publishing books and articles. These lay professors are not as immediately under ecclesiastical authority as priests are, but up to this point no great conflict has arisen regarding this matter.

Catholic biblical scholars bring to the text of Scripture the set of concerns and procedures that has been developed over the centuries among serious students of the Bible. In modern times this set of concerns is often called the historical-critical method. This approach takes as its primary task the understanding of the biblical text in its own time and on its own terms. It applies the powers of the mind to the text in order to understand it better and to appreciate it for itself. The major concerns of Catholic biblical scholarship can be presented under ten headings.

1. *Literary Criticism.* The Bible is basically an anthology of writings that bear witness to God's dealings with his people. In the Old Testament there are writings such as narratives, law codes, prophetic oracles, psalms, and wisdom books. In the New Testament there are stories of Jesus (the four gospels) and the early church (Acts) as well as epistles by Paul and other figures and an apocalypse (Revelation). Within these large literary types, there are also smaller forms such as sayings, parables, and exhortations. The Bible is most obviously a collection of pieces of

literature, and so the obvious starting point for any biblical scholar is literary criticism.

Literary criticism means applying to Scripture the questions and concerns used in the study of any literature. The aim behind the literary-critical approach to the Bible is not to reduce it to the level of other books, but rather to help us appreciate the ways in which the biblical writers communicated to their original audiences and still communicate to us today.

The first concern of literary criticism is with the words and images of the texts—the raw materials out of which any written communication is constructed. What does this or that word mean? Is the word being used literally or metaphorically? What symbolism is present in the passage? Then in a narrative text we want to know how the words are put together to form a story and how the characters in the story are related to one another. In a discourse or an epistle the literary critic focuses on the progress of thought—how the words and images are put together to form an argument or move people to good action. Obviously the literary critic proceeds from individual words and images to the coherence of the whole passage and then back to the words and images in light of the whole. This circularity inherent in the study of literature suggests that a text is always capable of receiving better and more adequate readings at various levels of understanding.

Literary critics are also concerned with the literary form of a text. The larger forms, or genres, in the New Testament are familiar: gospels, Acts, epistles, and Apocalypse. But within these larger forms the individual parts use vehicles like parables or proverbs or blessings and curses. The now familiar saying that "the medium is the message" makes the point that the choice of a specific literary mode of communication already begins the process of communication. The choice of the literary form of the personal resumé in the United States today communicates that the person is seeking a job. If the job applicant were to present the personnel manager with a poem or a slide show, his only hope for getting the job would be his display of ingenuity. Therefore, those who study Scripture from the perspective of literary criticism must attend to the literary forms used in the text and how the literary forms contribute to the expression of the message or content.

In one sense, literary criticism is the most basic approach to the biblical text and all the other methods are really specialized operations within this general method. But literary criticism in the narrow sense concentrates on the aesthetic appreciation of the biblical text as literature. Catholic biblical scholars generally have good literary educations and are naturally attracted to relating developments in literary criticism and literary theory to Scripture. The topic of many recent doctoral dissertations and journal articles by Catholics has been the literary outline or structure of a particular passage or biblical book. The dynamics and rhetorical techniques of narratives and the argument structure of the epistles have also been investigated by Catholic (and other) scholars. In parts of Europe and to some extent in the United States, Catholic scholars have tried to use structuralist analysis to understand biblical texts—that is, to go beneath the surface structures of the text and arrive at the deep structures of mind and reality.

The literary-critical work of Catholic biblical scholars is part of a larger movement in biblical scholarship that seeks a better appreciation of the Bible as story. This movement has also generated a broader theological approach—the so-called narrative theology or theology of story.

The problem connected with the literary approach is its tendency to reduce everything to textual aesthetics. Since the methods for interpreting fiction or poetry work well on various sections of Scripture, some conclude that everything in Scripture is fiction or poetry and thus without historical significance. Such a conclusion clearly goes beyond the boundaries of the Constitution on Divine Revelation and of Catholic theology in general. But it also raises an interesting question: If one admits that the Old Testament books of Jonah, Tobit, Esther, and Judith are literary fictions (and most Catholic biblical scholars take this approach—a correct approach, in my opinion), where does one draw the line between literary fiction and biblical history? This is a serious problem, but it should not obscure or detract from the very positive results that emerge from bringing to the text of Scripture the concerns and methods of literary criticism and appreciating the Bible as literature.

2. *Textual Criticism.* Since words are the materials out of which literary texts are constructed, it is essential to be as sure as possible about the accuracy of the words in the texts. The biblical texts have been handed on through the centuries and thus have been subject to distortion and human error. The goal of textual criticism is to get back as close as possible to what the biblical writers set down in their original manuscripts.

Reaching that goal is not easy. Textual critics must work with the Hebrew, Aramaic, and Greek manuscripts of the Bible. They must also make use of the earliest translations into Aramaic, Greek, Latin, Syriac, Ethiopic, Armenian, etc. Prior to the discovery of biblical manuscripts among the Dead Sea Scrolls of Qumran, the earliest available complete Hebrew manuscripts of the Old Testament were from the tenth and eleventh centuries A.D. The most important complete manuscripts of the New Testament came from the fourth and fifth centuries A.D., though there are some fragmentary manuscripts (the so-called papyri) from the second and third centuries. So textual critics must learn many ancient languages and prepare themselves to work with manuscripts far removed in time from the originals.

Having assembled the manuscript evidence, textual critics compare the texts to uncover textual variants. These variants are then weighed in order to determine on rational grounds what was the reading of the original text and what crept into the tradition as the result of conscious or unconscious alteration. In making such decisions, textual critics must take into account the quantity and quality of the manuscript evidence (external evidence) as well as the context, language, and style of the document (internal evidence). The task of the textual critic of the Bible is lightened somewhat by the general reliability of the process of transmission and the abundance of manuscript evidence.

A large amount of that manuscript evidence is preserved at the Vatican Library in Rome and in other libraries and monasteries of the Catholic church. These manuscripts are accessible to all scholars either for direct inspection or by photographic reproductions. Indeed the institutional structures of the Catholic church throughout the ages have made possible the transmission of the New Testament text from generation to generation, and our knowledge of the Old Testament tradition would be far poorer without these institutions.

Modern Catholic biblical scholars are well prepared for textual criticism through a good grounding in ancient languages. Nevertheless, few are prominent in this discipline. The most important exception is Carlo M. Martini, an Italian Jesuit who was a member of an international and interconfessional panel charged with preparing a new edition of the Greek New Testament. But he is now the archbishop of Milan, and his pastoral duties leave him little time for textual criticism. In a similar project for preparing a new edition of the Hebrew Old Testament, the Dominican scholar Dominique Barthélemy is a major figure. Several American Jesuits have worked with Frank M. Cross of Harvard in his reevaluation of Old Testament textual criticism in light of the Qumran discoveries.

The question remains: Why are so few Catholic scholars prominent in this discipline? The reason is clearly not lack of education, especially in the languages. One can only speculate on this matter, but perhaps one factor is a lack of the Protestant passion for discovering the exact wording of the original manuscript as it came from the hand of the biblical writer. Many evangelicals limit biblical inspiration to the so-called autographs (the manuscripts written by the biblical writer), and so there is a powerful religious motive to get back to the original texts. The Catholic doctrine of inspiration is not so narrow and places more trust in the process of transmission. Thus the divergent understandings of biblical inspiration may well be a factor here, though there are surely other factors: the pastoral demands made on Catholic clerics, the so-called "twentieth century interlude" in New Testament texual criticism, and the intrinsically difficult and often tedious nature of the research.

3. *The World of the Bible.* The heavy emphasis on biblical languages in the training of Catholic scholars finds expression most dramatically in research on the world of the Bible, especially on the texts discovered in the Middle East during the past two hundred years. These texts have allowed us to leap back over the centuries and to see what terms, ideas, and customs were in the background of the biblical writings.

For the Old Testament, the most important extrabiblical texts are in Semitic languages such as Akkadian, Aramaic, Ugaritic, and now Eblaite. These texts have illumined our understanding of the creation stories in Genesis, the historical setting of the biblical narratives from earliest times to the post-exilic period, and the language and literary form of the psalms. For the New Testament, the most significant ancient texts are in Hebrew, Aramaic, Greek, Latin, and Coptic (Nag Hammadi documents). These texts have shed light on the eschatological consciousness of the early Christians and the emergence of the early church, the cultural milieu(s) in which Christianity developed, and some of the problems and threats that it faced.

Many of these discoveries are so recent that they have still not been assimilated into biblical commentaries. When they are, it is crucial for the exegete to make clear what elements the biblical and extrabiblical texts share and where they differ. It is also important to specify the historical relationships between the two texts. Obviously the best parallels are those between texts from roughly the same time and place, for then we have a better chance of knowing what was "in the air."

The Biblical Institute Press of the Pontifical Biblical Institute in Rome has played a leading role in the editing and publishing of textual material from the ancient Near East. Many dissertations by Catholic scholars in Rome and elsewhere have been explorations of biblical texts in light of extrabiblical material. The professors at the Dominican Ecole Biblique in Jerusalem have been active participants in publishing the Qumran scrolls and in the archaeological excavations at Qumran and elsewhere. The faculty and students of the Studium Biblicum Franciscanum have made many contributions in the archaeology of early Christianity and in exploring the phenomenon of Jewish Christianity. Catholic scholars have been prominent in editing the texts from Ugarit, Qumran, and Nag Hammadi. The fact that many older Catholic scholars were well versed in the Greek and Latin classics has meant that the Greco-Roman setting of early Christianity has remained a lively field of research.

The great interest of Catholic scholars in the world of the Bible, and in texts from antiquity in particular, may stem in part from the perennial Catholic fascination with the relation between religion and culture. Catholic theology emphasizes the idea that God expresses himself in the midst of created realities and human culture. If this is so in the present, it must also have been so in antiquity when the books of the Bible were being composed. Therefore, the more that scholarship can reveal about the realities and culture of the biblical world, the richer and deeper will our understanding of the Bible be. My hunch is that this theological principle underlies much of the scientific research done by Catholic scholars on the world of the Bible.

4. *Word Study.* The serious training in biblical languages that is demanded of Catholic scholars also shows itself in their re-

search on the words and ideas in Scripture. The archaeological discoveries of recent years have brought forth many ancient texts, and those texts have greatly illumined our understanding of the languages of the Bible (Hebrew, Aramaic, and Greek). In Old Testament research, the Ugaritic texts from Ras-Shamra have revolutionized the study of Hebrew poetry, and the legal and mythic texts in Akkadian have made more intelligible various customs and terms in the Pentateuch. New Testament scholars have learned much about the kind of Greek used in Jesus' time from the Egyptian papyri and about the terminology and thought of Jewish apocalypticism from the Dead Sea Scrolls.

The most common kind of word study in the biblical field usually begins with a particularly important or problematic passage. In order to get a better understanding of a difficult word or idea in the target passage, the scholar makes a survey of the instances of the term in other documents. If a New Testament word is under consideration, then one looks at the Greek writings of the classical authors, the Greek translation of the Old Testament (Septuagint), and the Jewish authors Philo and Josephus. Naturally one also searches out the Hebrew Old Testament, the Dead Sea Scrolls, and other relevant documents. In each occurrence of the word, the focus of research is what it means in its context in the hope of understanding better the target passage.

In addition to the extrabiblical evidence, word study must also take into account parallels within the Bible itself. In this step an important change has taken place in Catholic biblical scholarship in recent years. In the past there was a tendency to join together all the biblical instances of a term or idea as if the Bible were made out of whole cloth. The theological assumption was that the Bible is a unity and that its language is a special type of Hebrew or Greek ("Holy Ghost Greek"). Now the major concern among Catholic scholars is to let the distinct accents within the Bible be heard. Their emphasis is on plurality of views within Scripture and on the particular contributions of the individual writers.

The phrase "biblical theology" is popular in Catholic circles, and a very common way of doing biblical theology is to trace the history of a word or idea from earliest Old Testament times, through intertestamental Jewish writings and classic works, to the New Testament. The aim is to see both continuity and decisive shifts in meaning; the conclusion to such studies usually involves a synthesis and an assessment of challenges for the church today. This kind of study places detailed philological research on individual biblical and extrabiblical texts in the broader framework of the history of biblical ideas.

Part of the popularity of this approach to biblical theology among Catholic scholars is due to the Catholic concern and fondness for tradition. This approach is really a charting out of the tradition of a biblical word or idea. For a church that is immersing itself more and more in language and ideas of Scripture, and that is so eager to hand on the tradition of faith, the concentration on key concepts and their development in biblical times and against the background of the biblical world is a sound approach and is sure to pay rich rewards.

5. *Source Criticism.* The task of detecting where a source was used in a biblical book is called "source criticism." Sometimes we are told explicitly by the biblical author that he was using a source, and so the procedure is quite simple. The more difficult instances are those in which the use of a source is suspected but needs to be proved by rational analysis. The internal criteria for determining the presence of a source in the Bible (or in any other text) include the following: vocabulary in a passage different from everything else in the book, a shift in tone or literary style, an unexpected interruption in the context and an awkward resumption of it later, the presence of the same story twice in slightly different forms, and theological or ideological contradictions within the same book.

The most important areas of source criticism in biblical research concern the Pentateuch and the synoptic gospels. The classic four-document hypothesis used in explaining the origin of the first five books of the Old Testament claims that Pentateuch is the fusion of four sources: Yahwist (J), Elohist (E), Priestly (P), and Deuteronomist (D). The time-span from the earliest document (J) to the latest (P) is about four hundred years (950 B.C. to 550 B.C.). The classic two-source hypothesis of the synoptic gospels maintains that Mark was the earliest gospel (ca. A.D. 70) and that Matthew and Luke (ca. A.D. 80–90) used both Mark and a collection of Jesus' sayings known among modern scholars as Q (ca. A.D. 50).

These hypotheses were popularized in liberal Protestant circles in nineteenth century Germany. The initial Catholic responses were generally suspicious and negative. But as the arguments and their proponents were gradually separated, there was increasing acceptance—to the point that both of these hypotheses are now part of "scholarly orthodoxy" among Catholic biblical scholars. In the broader context of biblical scholarship, both source-hypotheses are under attack, and Catholics can be found on the various sides of the debate. But there is some irony in the fact that the modern stronghold of the classic two-source hypothesis of the synoptic gospels is the Catholic University of Louvain in Belgium.

6. *Redaction Criticism.* Where it has been possible to isolate sources on external or internal grounds, the way is cleared for redaction criticism—the exegetical method that focuses on the particular emphases or views that the biblical writers have imposed on their sources. Besides the literary task of determining the final writer or redactor's distinctive contributions, redaction criticism also involves an historical task since the redactor's emphases and views can shed light on his situation within the early church and on the problems that the redactor and his community were facing.

It is possible to apply the techniques of redaction criticism to any part of Scripture, but the most fertile ground for redaction

criticism has been the synoptic gospels. The pioneers of the redaction-critical approach to gospel study (Günther Bornkamm,
Hans Conzelmann, Willi Marxsen) were German Protestant
scholars but their work in the late 1940s and 1950s was taken up
with great enthusiasm by Catholic scholars in the 1960s and
1970s. In one sense, the approach has been "played out," since
practically every gospel text has been the object of close redaction-critical analysis. On the other hand, the concern with the final redaction of biblical books has become so integral a part of the
exegetical task that no commentator can disregard it.

As I have already observed, redaction criticism is popular
among Catholic biblical scholars. This is so in part because Catholic scholars are part of the international and interconfessional
dialogue of biblical research today. But redaction criticism also
has had a special attractiveness for Catholics. The approach's understanding of the biblical writers as transmitters and interpreters of tradition strikes a responsive chord among tradition-
conscious Catholics. Its interest in early church life and its view
of the biblical authors as writing in and for particular communities of faith parallel the perennial Catholic concerns with the
church.

7. *Form Criticism.* Under the heading of literary criticism,
there was some discussion about the literary forms in which the
biblical writers expressed themselves and the extent to which the
choice of a particular literary form already communicates some
of the writer's message. Thus form criticism is really an aspect of
the general literary-critical task, and the first concern of the form
critic is to determine the literary form of the book (narrative, letter, etc.) or of the passages within a book (proverb, parable,
thanksgiving, etc.). But there is also an historical task in form criticism just as there is in redaction criticism. The assumption is that
the particular literary form can tell us something about the community in which the tradition was used and about the problems
that the community faced.

Catholic reactions to form criticism have been ambivalent. No one quarrels about the attention paid to literary forms. Indeed the determination of the literary forms has been strongly encouraged since *Divino Afflante Spiritu* (1943) and endorsed enthusiastically in Vatican II's Constitution on Divine Revelation (1965). The ambivalence involves the historical dimension. Catholics are generally positive toward the effort to get behind the texts into the life of the community. In fact, the historical program of form criticism has sometimes even been used apologetically to confirm the Catholic approach to the Bible as the church's book.

The Catholic problem with form criticism arises from the feeling that it is a poor historical tool. The attempt to construct the history of the early church on form-critical grounds has never been very successful. Where it has been tried, there has usually been a rather undisciplined mixing of form and content to arrive at tendentious (Martin Dibelius' phrase "in the beginning was the sermon") or skeptical conclusions about the relation of the tradition to Jesus of Nazareth (Rudolf Bultmann's history of the synoptic tradition). The tendency of the form-critical pioneers to overemphasize the creativity of the community at the expense of historical foundations went beyond the boundaries of Catholic theology and was sharply criticized.

8. *Historical Criticism.* The task of relating the texts of Scripture and the events behind them is called historical criticism. The term "historical-critical method" is generally taken to refer to the whole project of interpreting the biblical text in its historical setting and on its own terms. But "historical criticism" is also used in a narrower sense to describe the attempt to determine what really happened, for example, at Israel's escape from Egypt or on Easter Sunday morning. It was the hope of "scientific" historians in the nineteenth century to peel away the encrustations of tradition and arrive at the solid core of genuine history. In liberal Protestant circles in Germany there seems to have been an as-

out and is subordinated to tradition and the judgment of the ecclesiastical magisterium (the Pope and the bishops).[11]

Finally, the international character of the Catholic church is
hermeneutically significant.[12] The network of communication
that exists in the Catholic church will not allow North American
or Western European biblical scholars to avoid for long the challenges posed by third world exegetes. Indian Catholic scholars
have been exploring the relation between the historical-critical
approach to exegesis and the traditional Indian methods of interpreting religious texts. Latin American biblical theologians
have emphasized the centrality of the theme of liberation, the importance of being conscious of the life-setting of Bible study, and
the political significance of the biblical message in the past and today. Africans have discerned an affinity between the biblical
world and their own, and reject the idea that they must interpret
Scripture through the medium of Western culture. Feminists in
the United States have questioned the usual reconstruction of
early Christian history and found indications of a significant role
for women in early church life.

The following list of the methods and concerns of Catholic
biblical scholarship can summarize this part of the essay:

1. **Literary Criticism**
   What words, images, and symbols appear?
   What characters appear, and what are their relationships?
   What is the progress of thought?
   What literary form does the text have?
   How does the form contribute to expressing the content?

2. **Textual Criticism**
   Are there ancient variant readings?
   What can be explained away as unconscious or conscious al-
   terations?

What reading is demanded by the context, language, and style of the document?

3. **Parallels from the World of the Bible**
   What elements do the two texts have in common, and at what points do they differ or contradict one another?
   What is the historical relationship between the two texts?

4. **Word Study**
   Where else does the word appear, and what does it mean there?
   What meaning does it have in this context?
   Where does this instance stand in the term's history?

5. **Source Criticism**
   Did the document being studied have a source?
   What did that source say?
   How has the author used the source?

6. **Redaction Criticism**
   What unique views or unusual emphases does the author place on the sources?
   What is the author's life situation and theological outlook?

7. **Form Criticism**
   What is the literary form of the text?
   What does the literary form tell about the history of the community?

8. **Historical Criticism**
   What really happened?

9. **Translations**
   What text underlies the translation?
   What decisions did the translators have to make?
   What philosophy of translation is operative?
   Has anything been lost in translation?

10. **Meaning (Hermeneutics)**
    What does the text say?
    What do we bring to the text?
    What does it mean today?

By way of conclusion here, the method employed by the Latin American theologians of liberation deserves an explanation, for its principles differ from and challenge the historical-critical approach outlined in the preceding pages. The starting point for the liberation theologians is the analysis of contemporary sociopolitical experience, not the investigation of the ancient historical context. The life setting for this kind of biblical interpretation is the so-called base community, which arose as a popular movement in Catholicism. The biblical interpreters, whether they are peasants or professors, perceive clear parallels between the situation of people in Latin America today and that of God's people in biblical times. This parallelism leads back logically to the biblical texts as sources of enlightenment and encouragement today.

The liberation theologians also challenge the ideal of the historical critic as the objective spectator or the uninvolved reporter. About twenty-five years ago there was a lively debate among European and North American exegetes and theologians about whether it is possible to have presuppositionless exegesis. The answer, of course, is no. But nevertheless the aim of historical criticism is to put aside one's own presuppositions as much as possible and take the text on its own terms. The liberation theologians argue that this pseudo-objective stance merely masks a whole set of hidden and potentially destructive assumptions about God, humanity, and the world. Therefore they call for the interpreter's forthright admission of a political, sociological, or theological position. They criticize bitterly those learned biblical commentaries that issue from professors' desks, apparently untouched by social experience and devoid of human commitment.

The third challenge to historical criticism raised by the liberation theologians involves what constitutes the adequate interpretation of Scripture. The liberation theologians argue that intellectual appropriation is not enough. Neither is prayer enough. Rather, the biblical texts naturally lead to concrete social actions issuing from intellectual reflection and meditation. For these liberation theologians, biblical interpretation necessarily demands sociopolitical activity. Guided by the sophisticated hermeneutical theories of Paul Ricoeur, these liberation theologians speak of a hermeneutical circle that moves from suspicion about present-day experience ("something is wrong"), through suspicion about the ideologies and theologies (and exegesis) that support the present-day political structures, to the Bible as a source of faith and of inspiration for action, to action in the present time.

Thus the Latin American liberation theologians differ from the historical critics in their insistence on the present-day political situation as the starting point for biblical interpretation, their admission of presuppositions, and their emphasis on action as part of the interpretative process. Their approach is clearly open to abuses. But it does illuminate by contrast some of the major features of the historical-critical method. Also, there is still a place for historical criticism in liberation theology. The liberation theologians simply demand that other aspects of the interpretative process—present-day experience, the interpreter's presuppositions, and political action—be acknowledged and celebrated.

FROM DEATH TO LIFE (EPH 2:1–10)

The epistle to the Ephesians purports to be a letter written by Paul from prison. It is often classed with the epistles to the Philippians, Colossians, and Philemon as one of the captivity epistles. But most critical Catholic scholars now agree with their Protestant colleagues that Ephesians is an essay written by an admirer of Paul in the late first century A.D. (ca. A.D. 80–90) in order to emphasize the unity in Christ between Jewish Christians and Gentile Christians.[13] The case against Pauline authorship involves the more Semitic language and style of Ephesians, its different use of certain themes and motifs, and its divergent or more developed theology. The development of church structures assumed in the epistle and the problems facing the community are more easily linked with the late first century than the late 50s or early 60s. The hypothesis of non-Pauline authorship no longer presents a serious problem among Catholic exegetes (though a few still argue that Paul was the author).

Ephesians 2:1–10 deals with the reconciliation of sinful humanity to God. It prepares for the discussion of how non-Jews can become part of the people of God (Eph 2:11–22). The New American Bible translates the passage as follows:

> [1] You were dead because of your sins and offenses, [2] as you gave allegiance to the present age and to the prince of the air, that spirit who is even now at work among the rebellious. [3] All of us were once of their company: we lived at the level of the flesh, following every whim and fancy, and so by nature deserved God's wrath like the rest. [4] But God is rich in mercy; because of his great love for us [5] he brought us to life with Christ when we were dead in sin. By this favor you were saved. [6] Both with and in Christ Jesus he raised us up and gave us a place in the heavens, [7] that in the ages to come he might dis-

play the great wealth of his favor, manifested by his kindness to us in Christ Jesus. [8] I repeat, it is owing to his favor that salvation is yours, through faith. This is not your own doing, it is God's gift; [9] neither is it a reward for anything you have accomplished, so let no one pride himself on it. [10] We are truly his handiwork, created in Christ Jesus to lead the life of good deeds which God prepared for us in advance.

The Jerusalem Bible renders Ephesians 2:1–10 in this way:

[1] And you were dead, through the crimes and the sins [2] in which you used to live when you were following the way of this world, obeying the ruler who governs the air, the spirit who is at work in the rebellious. [3] We all were among them too in the past, living sensual lives, ruled entirely by our own physical desires and our own ideas; so that by nature we were as much under God's anger as the rest of the world. [4] But God loved us with so much love that he was generous with his mercy: [5] when we were dead through our sins, he brought us to life with Christ—it is through grace that you have been saved— [6] and raised us up with him and gave us a place with him in heaven, in Christ Jesus.
[7] This was to show for all ages to come, through his goodness towards us in Christ Jesus, how infinitely rich he is in grace. [8] Because it is by grace that you have been saved, through faith; not by anything of your own, but by a gift from God, [9] not by anything that you have done, so that nobody can claim the credit. [10] We are God's work of art, created in Christ Jesus to live the good life as from the beginning he had meant us to live it.

This summary of Paul's gospel first explains the state of sin and spiritual death in which the Gentile Christians lived before Christ (vv. 1–3). By their immoral actions they showed their allegiance to the powers of evil and thus deserved God's anger. Their lord was the "prince of the air," their way of life was guided by the "flesh," and their activities were sins and offenses.

Having described the negative period of their lives, the author of Ephesians develops the positive side in vv. 4–10. Through his most powerful display of mercy, love, and grace (vv. 4–5), God in Christ saved these Gentiles from their spiritual death and allowed them to share in the glory of the risen Lord (v. 6). The present aspect or realized aspect of eschatology is strongly emphasized: "you have been saved . . . he raised us up and gave us a place in the heavens." Nevertheless, the future aspect of eschatology ("in the ages to come") is not ignored (v. 7). There is so much emphasis on God in Christ as the source of salvation and the unmerited character of salvation (vv. 8–9) that one can suspect some controversy about this in the background of the letter. The passage closes in v. 10 with an exhortation to live the life that befits those whom God in Christ has saved. The second half of Ephesians (chaps. 4–6) spells out what such a life in conformity with salvation means.

I would like to comment on three matters arising from this extraordinarily rich text: its theology, its relationship to the genuine Pauline writings, and its transfer value.

The passage draws a contrast between what life for the Gentile Christians was before Christ (vv. 1–3) and what it is now (vv. 4–10). The most striking theological feature is the emphasis on salvation as already present (vv. 5–6), though the future dimension of salvation is also mentioned (v. 7). In this respect the language of Ephesians is stronger than that of Paul in Romans and Galatians. Another important feature is the stress on the unmerited nature of salvation (vv. 8–9) and the idea of good deeds flowing from God's gift of salvation (v. 10). Even though some

Protestants might think that Catholics seek salvation through works, the position of Catholic theology is perfectly consistent with Ephesians on this matter. These two themes—the present dimension of salvation and God's grace as the source of good deeds—would have great appeal to Catholic readers of the Bible.

How would Catholics assess the relationship of this passage to Paul's genuine letters? How would they evaluate the Ephesian emphasis on the presence of salvation in comparison to Paul's stress on the future dimension? Defenders of Pauline authorship of Ephesians would see it as the mature statement of ideas that were germinating in Galatians and Romans. Proponents of pseudonymous authorship would hold that it is an authentic development of Paul's thought for a new situation and time. The idea of using Galatians and Romans as a canon to criticize and judge other canonical writings would not be the usual approach for Catholics.[14] Instead of seizing upon the contradictions and differences, the first instinct of Catholics would be to focus on continuity and development. The aim behind charting the course of a Pauline theme like eschatology would be to illustrate growth in insight and ability to adapt the gospel to changed circumstances, not to let the power and majesty of the genuine Paul shine forth.

My final comment involves the hermeneutical transfer value of Ephesians 2:1–10. The text was clearly addressed to non-Jews who had turned from paganism to Christian faith. It deals with the experience of conversion ("once . . . but now"). The kind of conversion described implies that the converts were adults when they turned from paganism to Christianity, and in that turning experienced what is called "salvation." If one were to preach on this text today, the audience to whom it would mean most would be adults who had converted from paganism to Christianity. For Catholics and others baptized at infancy, this kind of conversion language is only partially appropriate. Even Christians baptized as adults but having been raised in Christian families and a Christian atmosphere will have not undergone the kind of experience sketched in Ephesians 2:1–10.

The problem of transfer is posed by the language of conversion leading to baptism found in this and other Pauline texts. Very often this conversion language is taken by committed Christians as something to be experienced anew everyday, as delineating the daily life of every Christian. This hermeneutical move transforms conversion language into maintenance language. I hesitate to use the word "distortion" because it is so strong. But at least Christians who use this text today should be aware of its original conversion setting in Ephesians and the only partly justified maintenance application they make of it.

SUMMARY

Since the Second Vatican Council, Catholics have been reading the Bible with enthusiasm and making it their own book. This development is especially dramatic in liturgy, religious education, and ecumenism. Vatican II's Constitution on Divine Revelation provided some helpful directions regarding the personal character of divine revelation, Scripture and tradition, the need for interpreting Scripture in its historical setting, respect for the Old Testament, recognition of the complexity of the gospels, and the Bible's place in church life.

Catholic biblical scholars bring to the Scriptures the questions and concerns that constitute the historical-critical method. They work in the areas of literary criticism, textual criticism, the world of the Bible, word study, source criticism, redaction criticism, form criticism, historical criticism, and translation. In interpreting the Bible, they are committed to ecumenism, maintain a strong sense of Catholic tradition, do their research in the context of today's church, and are participants in an international dialogue. A "Catholic" reading of Ephesians 2:1–10 emphasizes the present dimension of salvation and God's grace as the source of good actions, sees the passage as an authentic development of Paul's theology, and recognizes the limitations imposed by its original context as adult conversion leading to baptism.

NOTES

1. All quotations are from the translation by L. Walsh and W. Harrington in A. Flannery (ed.), *Vatican Council II: The Conciliar and Post-Conciliar Documents* (Northport, N.Y.: Costello, 1975) 750–65. For an excellent commentary on the document, see J.R. Donahue, "Scripture: A Roman Catholic Perspective," *Review and Expositor* 79 (1982) 231–44.

2. A helpful overview of problems is provided in T.A. Hoffmann, "Inspiration, Normativeness, Canonicity, and the Unique Sacred Character of the Bible," *Catholic Biblical Quarterly* 44 (1982) 447–69. The bibliography is very rich.

3. This paragraph summarizes the 1964 instruction of the Pontifical Biblical Commission; for a commentary on that document, see J.A. Fitzmyer, *A Christological Catechism: New Testament Answers* (Ramsey, N.J.: Paulist, 1982).

4. See my books, *Interpreting the New Testament: A Practical Guide* (New Testament Message 1; Wilmington, Del.: Michael Glazier, 1979) and *Interpreting the Old Testament: A Practical Guide* (Old Testament Message 1; Wilmington, Del.: Michael Glazier, 1981).

5. See the summary in E. Krentz, *The Historical-Critical Method* (Guides to Biblical Scholarship; Philadelphia: Fortress, 1975) 55.

6. See G.T. Montague, "Hermeneutics and the Teaching of Scripture," *Catholic Biblical Quarterly* 41 (1979) 1–17.

7. See my article, "The Ecumenical Importance of New Testament Research," *Biblical Theology Bulletin* 12 (1982) 20–23.

8. See P.-G. Müller, *Der Traditionsprozess im Neuen Testament: Kommunikationsanalytische Studien zur Versprachlichung des Jesusphänomens* (Freiburg-Basel-Vienna: Herder, 1982).

9. S.M. Schneiders, "Faith, Hermeneutics, and the Literal Sense of Scripture," *Theological Studies* 39 (1978) 719–36; "From Exegesis to Hermeneutics: The Problem of the Contemporary Meaning of Scripture," *Horizons* 8 (1981) 23–39.

10. S. Freyne, "Studying the Bible in an Ecumenical Context: A Roman Catholic Perspective," *Search* 5 (1982) 19–25.

11. A recent example is the ordination of women to the ministerial priesthood. The conclusion of a group of biblical scholars that Scripture presented no obstacle to women's ordination was deemed insufficient to justify departure from tradition by higher Roman authorities.

12. See my article, "Some New Voices in New Testament Interpretation," *Anglican Theological Review* 64 (1982) 362–70.

13. See Müller, *Der Traditionsprozess*, 245–46. This book contains a preface by Cardinal Joseph Ratzinger, the prefect of the Vatican's Congregation for the Doctrine of the Faith. It is clear that the modern Catholic approach to Christian origins does not demand a conservative attitude on authorship and date.

14. See my articles, "Ernst Käsemann on the Church in the New Testament," *Heythrop Journal* 12 (1971) 246–57, 367–78, for a discussion of Lutheran and Catholic views on this and related issues.

RECOMMENDED READINGS

Raymond E. Brown, *The Critical Meaning of the Bible* (Ramsey, N.J.: Paulist, 1981). Eight essays by a distinguished Catholic scholar on how the critical reading of the Bible can challenge Christians and the churches today.

Raymond E. Brown, Joseph A. Fitzmyer, and Roland E. Murphy (eds.), *The Jerome Biblical Commentary* (2 vols; Englewood

Cliffs, N.J.: Prentice-Hall, 1968). The collaborative effort of fifty North American Catholic scholars, this volume presents commentaries and general articles written from a modern critical perspective.

James T. Burtchaell, *Catholic Theories of Biblical Inspiration since 1810: A Review and Critique* (New York: Cambridge University Press, 1969). An examination of various Catholic viewpoints on whether and how the Bible is to be regarded as the infallible word of God.

Raymond F. Collins, *Introduction to the New Testament* (Garden City, N.Y.: Doubleday, 1983). An introduction to New Testament interpretation, which is distinctive for its comprehensiveness and its explicitly Catholic orientation.

George J. Dyer (ed.), *The Pastoral Guide to the Bible* (*Chicago Studies* 17/1; Mundelein, Ill.: Civitas Dei Foundation, 1978). Seven articles in question-and-answer format on the topics most relevant to the church's pastoral mission.

Joseph A. Fitzmyer, *A Christological Catechism: New Testament Answers* (Ramsey, N.J.: Paulist, 1982). The first part sets forth the biblical data on twenty questions in Christology, and the second part deals with the 1964 instruction of the Pontifical Biblical Commission on the historical truth of the gospels.

Daniel J. Harrington, *Interpreting the New Testament: A Practical Guide* (New Testament Message 1; Wilmington, Del.: Michael Glazier, 1979). This introduction to New Testament exegesis explains the methods described in the present essay and provides examples of how they can be used in studying specific biblical texts; *Interpreting the Old Testament: A Practical Guide* (Old Testament Message 1; Wilmington, Del.: Michael Glazier, 1981). The Old Testament equivalent of the book mentioned above.

Eugene LaVerdiere, *The New Testament in the Life of the Church: Evangelization, Prayer, Catechetics, Homiletics* (Notre Dame, Ind.: Ave Maria Press, 1980). An examination of the meth-

4

ods of communicative interpretation that are best suited to
pastoral activities.

James J. Megivern (ed.), *Bible Interpretation* (Official Catholic
Teachings; Wilmington, N.C.: Consortium Books/McGrath
Publishing Co., 1978). English translations of sixty-two documents, including Vatican II's Constitution on Divine Revelation, dealing with the place of the Bible in the church.

Bruce Vawter, *Biblical Inspiration* (Theological Resources; Philadelphia: Westminster, 1972). A comprehensive treatment of
inspiration as it has been understood from biblical times to
the present.

Grant R. Osborne

Evangelical Interpretation of Scripture

THE BACKGROUND TO CONTEMPORARY EVANGELICAL EXPOSITION

It is commonly believed among many non-evangelicals that fundamentalism-evangelicalism is a uniform tradition, characterized by a rigid, atomistic and static view of Scripture. Some have gone so far as to caricature the movement as a "nineteenth century heresy" which has no roots in the church before that time. For this reason it is important to realize that wide diversity exists within the camp and to understand the historical reasons why this should be so.

At the outset, I would assert that there are indeed historical roots for the evangelical doctrine of inerrancy, which means that the Bible is without error in its original autographs. Some among the evangelical tradition follow the commonly held view that inerrancy developed out of the application of Scottish Common Sense Realism to Scripture in the latter part of the nineteenth century. This philosophy stemmed from the inductive method propounded by Francis Bacon (1561–1626). It entailed an optimistic epistemology which assumed that definite apprehension of truth could be derived from an objective observation of facts. Therefore, one could ascertain with certainty the exact meaning of the Bible, which as divine revelation must be free from error. George Marsden argues that the Old Princetonians of the late nineteenth century (Charles Hodge, Archibald A. Hodge, Benjamin B. Warfield) forged their strong views on the basis of Common Sense Realism, "that the Scriptures not only contain, but ARE THE WORD OF GOD, and hence that all their elements and all their affirmations are absolutely errorless."[1]

However, John Woodbridge argues in response that Common Sense Realism was *a* formative factor but not *the* source of the doctrine. He states that while the Princetonians' view of inerrancy was reinforced by Baconianism (see above), their doctrine of complete infallibility was not "paradigm dependent" (i.e., it did not have its origin in) upon that perspective.[2] Indeed Woodbridge's work is a lengthy compilation of attitudes held by the church throughout church history toward Scripture. He asserts, validly I believe, that while the exact formulation of inerrancy or complete infallibility had not occurred earlier, the actual details were to be found earlier. Rogers and McKim (see note 1) and others had sought to demonstrate that the central position of the church had always been that infallibility was restricted only to religious or salvific concerns and that it was not extended to particular details such as historical or scientific statements. Woodbridge traces carefully the viewpoint of the church Fathers, the Reformers, and others, arguing that they primarily followed a view of complete infallibility. On this basis I would assert likewise that the fundamentalist/evangelical view of Scripture follows the central position which the church has held since the first century. Note carefully that I am not here arguing that this doctrine is *correct*, rather that it has historical precedent. The correctness of the position is yet to be discussed.

Modern   fundamentalism/evangelicalism,   however,   does have its primary roots in the late nineteenth and early twentieth centuries. Throughout most of the nineteenth century, America was basically conservative. In the post-Civil War era, in fact, it seemed that the conservative cause had indeed triumphed. Yet disquieting rumors continued to surface, primarily the pessimistic conclusions of higher criticism from Germany. These critical schools greatly influenced American scholarship. Ideas like Darwinian evolution and popular preachers like Henry Ward Beecher were harbingers in the 1870s of a movement which would soon cause a crisis and an intellectual revolution. It began in the universities and then spread to the pulpits. As conservative scholars retired they would be replaced by younger, more liberal thinkers, often educated on the Continent. Moreover, American conservatives were characterized more by practical piety than by apologetic concerns. The liberal preachers continued these pietistic emphases upon experience and morality as they sought to reconcile traditional views of Scripture with scientific views of reality. Preachers like Beecher and Lyman Abbott became exceedingly popular, and broader issues like the authority of Scripture were not truly understood.

The Evangelical Alliance, formed in 1846, became a major forum for debate. It centered upon revivalism, social concern (social justice, aid for the poor), sabbatarianism (the sacred nature of Sunday as the "Lord's day"), free enterprise, and a high view of biblical infallibility. In 1873 James McCosh, president of Princeton, attempted to make Darwinism and Scripture compatible and occasioned a vigorous debate. For the next three decades the emphasis shifted to higher criticism. In 1908 the Alliance became the Federal Council of Churches, still primarily conservative but moving steadily to the left.

The evangelical response to the threat was quite diverse. Some retreated into practical piety and refused to get involved in such issues. Dwight L. Moody, for instance, refused to address controversial questions and simply preached personal repentance and the gospel. He believed that if one ignores error, it will pass away. Here he alluded to Gamaliel's advice in Acts 5:38–39: "Therefore, in the present case I advise you: Leave these men alone! Let them go! For if their purpose or activity is of human origin, it will fail. But if it is from God, you will not be able to stop these men; you will only find yourselves fighting against God." Many others, however (including direct associates of Moody's like Reuben Torrey), believed in direct confrontation. The term "fundamentalist" arose from a series of twelve volumes published between 1910 and 1915, *The Fundamentals*, though the title was first used by Curtis Lawes in 1920. These were written by conservative scholars to uphold the traditional views regarding the Bible and the cardinal tenets of the faith against the encroaching conclusions of "higher criticism" (e.g., denying the traditional authorship and dates of biblical books, questioning that Jesus actually uttered the "sayings" attributed to him in the gospels) and evolution. These volumes dispel the commonly held view that fundamentalism arose out of an anti-intellectual milieu. Indeed they attempted to "beat the higher critics at their own game," asserting that "higher criticism was not critical enough."[3]

One of the basic debates between fundamentalism and nonfundamentalism concerned Bible study methods. The results of Common Sense Realism on the growing conservative movement lay in the denial of critical tools and the assertion that knowledge of biblical truth was open to the average person utilizing only his Bible and with the aid of the Holy Spirit. Proof-texting, the practice of proving a doctrinal point by alluding to a scriptural text, was deemed sufficient to establish a particular viewpoint. One of the most popular works in this regard was Reuben Torrey's *What the Bible Teaches* (1898), which claimed to be both "unbiased" and "scientific" as it documented (in five hundred pages) theological statements with biblical proof-texts. The inductive method of Bible study, proceeding synthetically from the whole to the parts and seeking to elucidate major themes, came into prominence during this period. The term "inductive study" in fundamentalism came to be used for that method which studied the text by itself rather than utilizing critical tools or commentaries to elucidate its meaning. Yet it would be shallow to hint that this was the only method. Conservatives like J. Gresham Machen and Ned Stonehouse continued to interact with the highest levels of scholarship throughout this era. However, the synthetic method did predominate.

Two further aspects should be noted. First, fundamentalism received impetus from a series of Bible conferences between 1876 and 1910. These centered upon both prophecy and apologetics, attempting to demonstrate the "true faith" and to warn against the coming "apostasy" (2 Thess 2:3) which was identified with the rising liberal movement. The most important was the 1895 conference in Niagara, New York. It adopted the five-point platform which later became the basis of *The Fundamentals:* the inerrancy of the Bible, the virgin birth, the deity of Christ, the substitutionary atonement (the view that Jesus died as the sacrifice or "substitute" for man's sins), and the physical resurrection of Christ and his second coming.

Second, the gradual control which non-conservatives established over the nation's higher institutions of learning led to the Bible Institute movement. As their influence waned in the major seminaries, fundamentalists developed their own schools in which the Bible was the core of the program. Their purpose was to prepare church leaders rather than to provide a broad-based education. Therefore, they eschewed the arts in favor of biblical and practical courses like pastoral care or Christian education (yet without educational theory derived from the universities). However, this movement was not so much a retreat from society as it was an attempt to preserve the Bible-based education of the past. This came to a head in 1929, when J. Gresham Machen and Robert Dick Wilson resigned from Princeton and created a new school, Westminster Theological Seminary, in Philadelphia. From that time the separation was fairly complete, and for the next two decades there was little dialogue between the liberal and fundamentalist factions.[4]

One event which illustrates the growing rift was the so-called "monkey trial" in 1925 of John Scopes, a teacher of evolution in Dayton, Tennessee. The scene, trumpeted around the world by the press, pitted William Jennings Bryan, golden-tongued orator and four-time candidate for president of the United States, against the leading trial lawyer of his day, Clarence Darrow. The results are too well known to chronicle: Darrow not only demolished Bryan's arguments but also humiliated his views. From that time, fundamentalism was increasingly considered a backward, reactionary, and anti-intellectual bastion of rural Protestantism.

The ensuing years saw two developments within fundamentalism: a diminution of influence in broad sectors of American life and increasing infighting among themselves. In the years of *The Fundamentals* there was a sense of unity among the Reformed, Wesleyan, and millenarian segments. In fact, we must correct the hyperbolic statements of Sandeen and others that fundamentalism was a millenarian or dispensational movement (the view that biblical history proceeded via periods or "dispensations" within which God attempted in various ways to bring mankind back into fellowship with himself). While this faction has become predominant among current fundamentalists, the origins of the movement were complex and included an amalgamation of many traditions. However with the increased controversies within each group, they lost contact with one another and in the 1930s began splitting into factions within themselves.[5] The concern for theological precision began to extend to peripheral as well as cardinal tenets of the faith, and denominational splits multiplied, often over the issue of separation (from Christian groups not deemed sufficiently orthodox). Of course, there were more than doctrinal differences behind these wars. In a time of controversy, many strong-willed, charismatic individuals came to the forefront. The power plays among these leaders also caused many of the splits. It is fair to say that most of the vast number of small denominations today came into being in the late 1920s or the 1930s.

These internal conflicts as well as the poor image of fundamentalism caused it to lose public visibility and influence during the 1930s.[6] However, it would be erroneous to conclude that it was dying during those years. Statistics, in fact, show that it continued to grow, partly from the influx of immigrant groups who aligned themselves with fundamentalist concerns and partly from many Americans who grew disenchanted with the mainstream denominations. Nevertheless, discouragement was the order of the day within fundamentalism, primarily because they had no national voice but also because the splits had made the splinter groups small, ineffective units which could not perceive the growth occurring within the scene as a whole. Moreover, the polemical, reactionary mind-set which predominated was not attuned to optimism, that is, they centered upon the negative aspects of the movement and could not perceive the larger picture.[7]

In the 1940s a new group began to emerge, now known as "evangelicalism." It differed from militant fundamentalism along several lines: (1) a desire to dialogue with the world of scholarship, (2) a disavowal of radical separation (i.e., the view that one had to separate oneself from any group or person not espousing the "party line" in its details as well as in its essentials), (3) a greater theological openness on peripheral matters, for instance on eschatological issues, (4) cooperative evangelism, seen especially in the Billy Graham crusades in the 1950s, (5) a more eclectic education, as seen in the formation of Fuller Seminary in 1947, (6) a refusal to align flag-waving, political conservativism with orthodoxy, and (7) social concern, for instance the development of missionary agencies which primarily dealt with world relief and medical problems.

There are now two basic factions within the ultra-conservative camp, namely the fundamentalist and the evangelical. The major issue which distinguishes the two is separation, which entails a more wholistic set of attitudes regarding the Christian's relationship to the world and other Christian groups. In many cases the use of the Bible is very similar, especially on the popular level. Both groups tend to proof-text and to atomize Scripture (see further below). Yet with respect to external aspects they differ markedly. The fundamentalists tend to take a negative approach to other Christian groups and to such "worldly" amusements as movies, cards, dancing, etc. Moreover, they are often characterized by "second-degree separation," i.e., severance not only from the world of liberalism but also from evangelicals who refuse to detach themselves from such. The classic example is the fundamentalist opposition to Billy Graham because of his openness to "liberal" participation in his crusades. The evangelical, on the other hand, is more open to such things as movies or recreation on Sunday. Furthermore, there is a desire to dialogue with other Christian movements and to cooperate where such does not compromise the basic tenets of evangelical dogma (on which see above). Evangelicals participate in the Society of Biblical Literature and attend meetings of the National Council of Churches (although there is great debate regarding the extent of participation in the latter).

The break between the two can be seen, for instance, in the rival national organizations. In September 1941, Carl McIntire formed the American Council of Christian Churches (ACCC) and in October of that year another conference was held at Moody Bible Institute to form the National Association of Evangelicals. The former organization specifically wished to combat the Federal Council of Churches while the latter did not demand that their members sever all ties. While the two groups had quite similar views with respect to Scripture and other doctrines, they differed greatly in terms of attitudes toward outsiders (see the previous paragraph).

However, other splinter movements within the two groups have occurred. Fundamentalism has seen several splits, for example that between McIntire and Bob Jones. Jerry Falwell has been moving more toward the evangelical camp in his rhetoric, although many of his political statements are geared to the fundamentalist.[8] The ACCC split a few years ago between a moderate faction and a McIntire-led splinter group. The current organization is controlled by the moderates.

Evangelicalism is also divided, primarily on the issue of inerrancy. The debate has been chronicled in the two works of Harold Lindsell,[9] which unfortunately are highly polemical. The Evangelical Theological Society, organized in 1949 to provide an eclectic forum for theological discussion, has made inerrancy its only doctrinal statement so as to provide a platform for differences on other matters. In recent years, however, it has been divided on a definition and criteria for inerrancy. As a result, another organization, the International Council on Biblical Inerrancy (ICBI), has been formed to adjudicate a more carefully defined statement on the issue. Those who affirm the doctrine of total infallibility/inerrancy are now subdivided into two further groups, one segment seeking to establish criteria for deciding what affirms the doctrine and another wishing to allow flexibility in determining details.

This, of course, is not to intimate that inerrancy is the sole or even the major dividing factor among evangelicals. Many other factors (e.g., high versus low forms of worship, eschatological views, the charismatic issue, the sacraments, women in the church, ethical issues, Calvinism versus Arminianism versus Anabaptism) could be mentioned. However, inerrancy most clearly relates to the use of Scripture and currently is a major contention. The 1982 meeting of the Evangelical Theological Society

(December 15–17, 1982) centered upon "biblical criticism" and concluded with a basic affirmation of critical tools when used moderately, i.e, as a means of interpreting a passage rather than determining the degree of authenticity.

THE EVANGELICAL AND SCRIPTURE

As one might determine from the preceding discussion, there is wide diversity among evangelicals with respect to their use of Scripture. Many segments of the various camps do indeed employ an atomistic, proof-texting approach and strongly disparage the use of tools like commentaries or background literature, saying that they invariably focus upon problems of interpretation and inevitably move one away from a commitment to the "simple gospel." This relic of "common sense realism" is still prevalent. However, the interest in a proper approach to the Bible is certainly growing, as witness the recent upsurge in evangelical works on Bible study methods or hermeneutics. To be certain, many books go no further than inductive Bible study. However, others are extremely sophisticated and aware of the enormous body of literature, secular and religious, on the problem of literary interpretation. J. Robertson McQuilkin, president of Columbia Bible College, says, "Even an introductory textbook on hermeneutics ought to be . . . thoroughly grounded in solid scholarship. . . ."[10] It is very clear that McQuilkin and others deny the validity of proof-texting. Walter Kaiser states that " 'prooftexting,' the isolation and use of verses apart from their immediate or sectional content, is reprehensible and should be discontinued immediately."[11] Recent graduates of evangelical schools have had strong courses in proper exegetical procedure.

1. *Meaning and the Author-Text-Reader Problem.* Evangelicals traditionally stress "what it meant" as well as "what it means." There is strong unanimity with respect to intentionality, i.e., the possibility of recovering the author's intended meaning. The

modern hermeneutical dilemma stems from the relation between author, text and reader, that is, the difficulty of pre-understanding, of moving behind one's own pre-conceived notions to enter into the thought-world of the text. When one goes the next step and seeks to discover the author's intended meaning, the task becomes immeasurably more complex. As a result many literary schools posit the autonomy of the text from the author and to a greater or lesser degree pronounce the impossibility of ascertaining the "author's intended meaning." Instead, the focus has shifted to the reader, and theories of "polyvalence" or "multiple meanings" predominate. As one enters the world of the text, a hermeneutical circle occurs in which both text and reader are altered. While total subjectivity does not result, the dynamic transference of meaning allows many possible interpretations to occur depending on the context or perspective of the reader.[12]

While recognizing the thorny problems involved in the task of interpretation, evangelicals are not so pessimistic regarding the task of determining the intended meaning. While there is no space to present detailed arguments, I might mention a few salient points. At the outset, the work of the literary critic E.D. Hirsch has become very popular. Building upon Wittgenstein's theory of "family resemblances" between "language games," Hirsch argues that understanding is connected to "intrinsic genre," that is, the "type of utterance" which narrows down the "rules" that apply to a particular speech. While pre-understanding plays a major role in interpretation, there is a basic genre which is intrinsic to a literary work and which, when discovered, can lead to a correct delineation of its original, intended meaning.[13]

Hirsch separates meaning (what it meant) and significance (what it means) into two separate aspects of the hermeneutical task. The issue is whether one can get behind the latter to the former. After lengthy discussion of the problem of semantics and meaning, Moises Silva is convinced that one can: "I take it as a valid assumption that the interpreter approaches any text with a multitude of experiences . . . that inform his or her understanding of that text. . . . But I believe just as strongly that the interpreter may *transcend,* though not eliminate, that point of reference. . . . The moment we look at a text we contextualize it, but a self-awareness of that fact opens up the possibility of modifying our point of reference in the light of contradictory data."[14]

A connected issue relates to the questions of biblical authority and propositional revelation in Scripture, i.e., that the Bible is the actual Word of God in propositional form rather than a witness to God's revelation. Paul Achtemeier asserts that a concern for an infallible, propositional revelation has led to the type of harmonizing (in order to solve discrepancies) which in effect is self-contradictory, since it creates more problems than it solves.[15] He therefore proposes a dynamic model which views inspiration as a process involving not only the original tradition but later situations and respondents. Interestingly, the type of "glib harmonization" which Achtemeier attacks is also denied by Donald A. Carson, who nevertheless argues further that the method when utilized as one among many literary tools can be highly useful.[16]

To return to the subject of propositional revelation, Wayne Grudem provides an extensive discussion of Scripture's "self-attestation," arguing (1) that all of the Old Testament writings are considered God's words, (2) that the written words of God have the same truth-status as the spoken words of God, and (3) that the New Testament writings attained the same status as the Old Testament writings.[17] He concludes this after examining introductory formulas and claims to authority within the biblical text. The implications are crucial for the evangelical claim to propositional revelation. If Grudem's findings are correct, the Bible claims to *be* the Word of God, not only to testify to the Word of God. Moreover, the Bible would demand to be understood in terms of its original meaning, not merely be open to multiple meanings in various contexts. This is at the heart of the evangelical view of

Scripture. I also concur with Anthony C. Thiselton's excellent discussion of authority and the Bible's "language games." He argues that both static and dynamic views are valid: The Bible is more than "a handbook of information and description" in that it embraces a "whole range of dynamic speech-acts"; yet at the same time this performative element rests "on the truth of certain states of affairs in God's relation to the world."[18] Few evangelicals would argue for a purely static view of Scripture. Most would see both static and dynamic elements, which we might align with meaning and significance.

2. *Literary Criticism.* The first stage of evangelical criticism obviously deals with the larger questions of genre, plot, narrative structure, and thought development. The best control over the tendency to atomize individual statements is constant cognizance of the entire context within which assertions are found. Thus serious Bible study begins with rhetorical criticism, the study of the logical patterns which characterize the total message. Hermeneutic texts center specifically upon genre, covered under the rubric "special revelation." However, it is seldom wholistic, for while traditional aspects like figures of speech, parables, and apocalyptic are discussed, there is seldom coverage of gospels or narrative hermeneutics. An excellent work which rectifies this is *How To Read the Bible for All Its Worth* by Gordon D. Fee and Douglas Stuart, with successive chapters on the basic genres: the epistles, Old Testament narratives, Acts, the gospels, parables, the law(s), the prophets, the psalms, wisdom, and Revelation.

Genre has come increasingly to the fore in recent debates on the gospels. Not only has a plethora of works appeared on the gospel genre, but also it has led to several studies purporting to interpret the gospel narratives on the basis of generic considerations. This may best be exemplified by the recent Matthew commentary by Robert Gundry.[19] He states that the Matthean portions of this gospel (e.g., the magi) are not historical but are "creative midrash," Jewish fictional pieces which were meant to be interpreted as such by his Jewish audience. However, many feel that Gundry has not defined midrash properly nor has he applied proper parallels. Genre must first be identified correctly and then the characteristics must be drawn adequately between the pieces of literature.

Once the genre has been isolated, an ever-narrowing series of concentric approaches delves deeper and deeper into the text. Here the evangelical hermeneutic demonstrates an affinity with modern trends, as recent schools (e.g., structuralism, canon criticism, rhetorical criticism) have moved away from a stress on the parts (the error of form criticism) to the centrality of the whole. Literary criticism assumes that the "world of text" as well as historical-critical concerns is a valid source for study. The symmetry of the final product therefore is a primary focus, and evangelical approaches have historically stressed this contextual aspect. Interestingly, the major Bible study approach stemming from the "Common Sense Realism" school at the turn of the century was the synthetic method described in James Gray's *How To Master the Bible* (1904), which assumed the priority of the whole.[20]

This remains the core of modern-day inductive methodology, which begins by charting the whole structure of a book, delineating the pattern of its argumentation and its major themes. Without the sophisticated study of compositional techniques exhibited in the world of academia, the inductivist still seeks the interplay of narrative factors in the text. Evangelical scholars are more and more being trained in literary theory and producing works in this field. Yet the so-called "fictive" (rhetorical schools argue that all narratives have the basic elements of "fiction," i.e., plot, structure, character, conflict) components stemming from the school of narrative hermeneutics are strongly criticized for the facile assumptions regarding the aesthetic element of Scripture. Evangelicals would want to restrict fictive factors to that genre rather than extend them to historical and didactic portions of the Bible. With respect to parables, for instance, the evangelical would utilize modern parable research regarding the complexity of the interpretive task but would still seek the "single meaning" of the parable in its setting as opposed to the multiple meanings attributed by structuralists.[21]

3. *Textual Criticism.* Evangelicals, with their stress on the propositional content of Scripture, are naturally very concerned to ascertain the original words of the biblical text. The description of the task by Professor Harrington above is very similar to that employed by evangelicals. Issues, however, are slightly different. One major debate between fundamentalists and evangelicals centers upon the *textus receptus,* the "received text" developed by Erasmus and that behind the King James Bible. Those behind the "King James only" movement argue for the "majority text," i.e., the text supported by the majority of the ancient manuscripts. However, since most exemplars copied before A.D. 800 have been destroyed, the majority of evangelical scholars accept the eclectic method developed by Westcott and Hort rather than the "received text."

In spite of the commitment to the text, however, there is also a paucity of evangelical text-critics. Many have done text-critical research in their doctoral work, largely due to the fact that several graduate programs will not allow exegetical studies from an evangelical perspective. However, few follow up this program with further text-critical research. The reasons given by Professor Harrington for the poor state of textual criticism in Catholic circles apply also to the evangelical situation.

4. *The Historical-Critical Method.* There is a great debate in both evangelical and non-evangelical circles regarding the validity of historical-critical research. The pessimism of the approach and the absence of constructive results have made scholars from many traditions leery about its value. However, one must differentiate various aspects of a particular method and avoid labeling the entire school by its negative characteristics. This is the debate

within evangelicalism at the present time. Both form and redaction criticism have been closely identified with tradition criticism, which tends to determine the authenticity of a pericope or story on the basis of its form. If the saying or story is simple rather than complex, it is more likely to be authentic, that is, to stem from the historical Jesus rather than the later church. These scholars theorize that the needs of the church were read back onto the lips of Jesus. Tradition critics tend to determine the authenticity of Jesus' sayings in the gospels on the basis of three criteria:[22] (1) dissimilarity, which assumes that a saying is authentic only if it cannot be paralleled either in Judaism or in the early church, (2) multiple attestation, which views a saying/pericope as authentic if it can be traced through several sources or layers of tradition, and (3) coherence, which accepts a tradition that is consistent with passages which have already been authenticated. However, the philosophical skepticism behind these has been challenged from many quarters, and the approach is unacceptable to evangelicals.

Some believe that such methodological problems belie the method as whole.[23] They argue for an historical-theological rather than a historical-critical method on the grounds that the former is in closer proximity to the biblical view of itself. The reconstruction of the "original event" is viewed as a speculative enterprise which can never provide a constructive alternative to the text as it is. Others, like the canon critics, accept the criticisms but assert that one must not take a "naive" approach to the text. Evangelicalism is divided on the issue, although I admit that I stand more closely to the latter position.

Redaction criticism is a case in point. While form criticism sought the *Sitz im Leben* or social matrix from which various strata of tradition stemmed, redaction criticism has studied the final author's contribution. In so doing, many critics have assumed that only those segments peculiar to an individual evangelist carry his imprimatur. However, such a supposition lacks proof, for the biblical writers used the traditions themselves as well as additions/omissions in presenting their messages. Moreover, most evangelicals are not so settled on the classical form of the documentary hypothesis (Matthew and Luke utilizing Mark and Q) that they will build entire edifices of interpretation upon it. While it is commonly accepted as a working hypothesis, few would wish to make it the core of redaction-critical research. Therefore, both in terms of tradition and source criticism, there is a degree of antipathy toward a full-blown redactional program.

Nevertheless, at a recent ETS (Evangelical Theological Society) meeting (1982) the basic approach was affirmed. The theological goals of redaction criticism parallel both rhetorical criticism (in the centrality of structure) and biblical theology (in the delineation of the individual author's message). Indeed, the basic desire to protect the author's intended meaning is best fulfilled by redaction criticism, which accents the final form over the separate traditions. For these reasons there is a growing affirmation of a nuanced methodology within evangelicalism. In similar fashion, a carefully controlled historical-critical method is strongly questioned but not negated, and the questions addressed to it are very similar to those asked by the broader spectrum of scholarship.

5. *Biblical Backgrounds.* Disciplines which uncover data bearing upon biblical history and customs have always been represented heavily in the evangelical school. The concern for the exact meaning of the text naturally leads to an emphasis upon the fields of archaeology, ancient languages, and history. At times there have been hasty conclusions drawn regarding the apologetic value of such finds as Jericho or the Hittites, and careful scholars now proclaim correctly that the primary value of archaeology is descriptive (providing data for understanding the biblical world) rather than apologetic (proving the historical reliability of accounts), since results are so tentative.[24] However, the

value of such discoveries is immense, and our knowledge of the biblical world has increased dramatically in recent years.

There are several criteria for deciding when an extrabiblical parallel may be adduced in elucidating a text: (1) Do not assume that any thematic link constitutes a genealogical relationship. History-of-religions scholars have often assumed that Hellenistic parallels were superior to Jewish parallels; one must see which more closely elucidates the text. (2) Make certain that it comes from the same period; the mystery religions, for instance, stem from a later period and cannot be behind such New Testament practices as baptism. Also talmudic evidence has often been used too casually without asking whether it truly stemmed from the pre-A.D. 70 Jewish situation. (3) Work not only with the current situation at the time of writing but also with the historical development behind it. Intertestamental allusions are critical for understanding the mind-set of the New Testament writers. (4) Be wholistic in your search. We can no longer assume that either Judaism or Hellenism is solely responsible for New Testament ideas, nor that Canaanite practices are responsible for Old Testament development. Recent studies have shown how cosmopolitan the ancient world actually was. (5) Look at wording and style. If the connection is no more than conceptual, it is possible but less likely than if one can denote an allusion to the parallel piece. (6) If differences outweigh similarities, one should consider other options. Preliminary theories regarding the influence of Qumran on the New Testament (e.g., with Jesus or John the Baptist) have been discarded because the similarities were overdrawn.

Most importantly, historical background is deemed absolutely critical for a proper understanding of the text. The evangelical demand for propositional truth has always produced a great desire to determine the literal meaning of Scripture. This cannot be done adequately without applying the background behind the biblical statements, for one must recognize the analogical nature of biblical language and the cultural gap between it and our day. To overcome that gap, historical data is a critical need.

6. *Semantics and Grammar.* Most evangelical schools still require Greek and Hebrew, and the biblical languages are deemed necessary for proper interpretation. The classical tenets of grammatical-syntactical exegesis are at the heart of the hermeneutical task. Students are required to study arduously the classical grammars such as Blass-Debrunner-Funk, Moulton-Hope-Turner, Zerwick and Moule for Greek, or Gesenius-Kautzsch, Hartmann, and Lambdin for Hebrew. Moreover, the cognate languages such as Akkadian, Sumerian, Ugaritic, and Aramaic are taught to those who wish to specialize. In fact, Trinity is one of the centers developing an exciting new tool for grammatical research, called GRAMCORD, i.e., a Grammatical Concordance for the biblical languages employing computer programming. The grammatical configuration of the entire New Testament in Greek has been coded into the computer, and similar programs are in process for the Hebrew Old Testament as well as for the Septuagint and such extrabiblical literature as Josephus and Philo. Grammatical configurations can now be traced with precision and speed, and students in our advanced grammar course are already reworking major grammatical concepts. Judging from the growing number of SBL (Society of Biblical Literature) seminars and papers on this topic, this is clearly one of the major movements for the next decade.

Lexicography, the meaning of individual words and concepts, is also receiving new impetus in our day. The number of tools available for word studies has risen remarkably, and highly sophisticated studies along the lines of James Barr's classic *Semantics of Biblical Language* (1961) are readily available. In addition to the ten-volume *Theological Dictionary of the New Testament,* there is the well-written three-volume *New International Dictionary of New Testament Theology* and many similar works. While to an ex-

tent many fall into Barr's criticism of "illegitimate totality transfer" (i.e., the tendency to read the whole theology behind a
concept into individual uses of a term), there is evidence for a
growing appreciation for proper lexical techniques (e.g., Silva's
work in note 14).

One major improvement lies in the use of parallels. In the
past it has been common to read any possible parallel passage
into the meaning of an individual statement. Thus there would
be articles on the Essene background of the incarnational theology of Hebrews 2 alongside articles on the Hellenistic origin of
that passage. Now there is a greater tendency to differentiate
seeming parallels from true parallels. No longer can we interpret
James' discussion of faith and works simply on the basis of Paul's
teaching. Now we must examine the semantic linkage and the
contextual meaning in both contexts before we establish connective lines between the two. I believe that the differences outweigh
the similarities and that therefore we cannot establish a valid link
between Paul and James.

The evangelical heritage, from A.T. Robertson and J.B.
Lightfoot at the turn of the century to F.F. Bruce and I. Howard
Marshall today, has always shown primary interest in this aspect
of hermeneutics. The minutiae of the text have always had a particular fascination for evangelical preachers, as witness the number of years Martin Lloyd-James spent preaching on Romans or
James Montgomery Boice on the gospel of John. This of course
is intimately connected to the view of Scripture, but it also is seen
in the concomitant demand for accuracy, that is, the need to understand the parts before expounding the whole.

7. *Biblical Theology and Systematic Theology.* The question of
unity and diversity in the Bible has long fascinated scholars. Recently it has come to the fore in the debate on the validity of systematic theology. The Reformers stressed the principle of
analogia fidei, the interpretation of individual portions of Scripture on the basis of other portions. Since the rise of the biblical

theology movement in Germany in the eighteenth century, this principle has been under attack. The diverse emphases of individual portions of the Bible have so been stressed that any possibility of attaining a unified field of meaning which cuts across the differences has often been rejected as an impossible task. Theology, it is now being said, is descriptive rather than normative.

Evangelicals have always rejected this dichotomy as unnecessary (see Carson's article in note 16). The basic unity is not a given, for it must be demonstrated. Diversity is certainly present between the documents. Yet this diversity does not rule out of hand the unity, and scholars argue that an interpreter can amalgamate individual statements into "covering models" which unify the diverse approaches to an issue into an overall biblical theology. Evangelicals would seek to maintain diversity (biblical theology) and yet to determine the underlying unity behind it (systematic theology). To stress the diversity at the expense of the unity is reductionistic; to stress the unity and ignore the diversity is speculative and subjective. When one goes beyond the surface language to the underlying concepts, the diverse statements are often seen to be compatible.

Nevertheless, one cannot ignore the surface meaning and "proof-text" dogma. It is also increasingly recognized that isolated biblical statements do not state dogmatic truths as much as apply aspects of the larger truth to circumstantial needs in the community addressed by the book. Dogma is determined by a complex process. First, one notes all the biblical passages which address a particular topic and exegetes those passages in terms of their original, intended meaning. Herein one notes tremendous diversity of emphasis and expression.

Next, the theologian begins the task of compilation. First, he or she elucidates the biblical theology of books and then authors on this topic. Second, one determines the larger unity within major traditions, e.g., the partriarchal/monarchical or prophetic periods in the Old Testament or the Palestinian or Gentile mission periods of the New Testament. Third, the full-fledged doctrine is traced through the biblical period, noting shifts of interest and the progress of revelation in salvation-history. This occurs under the aegis of biblical theology. Finally, the systematic theologian takes this data, seen in its diversity and unity, and restates it along the lines first of the history of dogma and second of the cultural expressions of the current age. In short, he or she reworks the biblical material so that it may be understood logically, in its whole and in its parts, by the modern person.

8. *Contextualization.* We have moved from "what it meant" (the task of exegetical theology and biblical theology) to "what it means" (the task of systematic theology and homiletical theology). Contextualization, the heremeneutical side of homiletical theology, is the final step, linked with the task of proclamation. The theory has been developed by missiologists who are concerned for cross-cultural communication. Evangelicals, historically linked to pietistic and revivalist concerns, have always stressed this aspect. Contextualization says that the task of interpretation is never complete until one has wedded the exegesis of the Word to an exegesis of the world. The debate on this issue centers upon the interface between the two spheres. If the Word of God is propositional, one can "contextualize" the form but not the content of the biblical message. If it is functional (see note 12), the current context would control the interpretation and one would develop an "indigenous theology" (the claim of the liberation theologian, for instance). The evangelical has always argued for the former stance.

The first stage of contextualization concerns the question of normative versus cultural interpretation. The interpreter asks whether the biblical command or principle is totally linked to the cultural situation (e.g., Paul's urban-centered evangelism at Ephesus in Acts 19) or whether the teaching transcends the circumstances and is normative for all ages (e.g., the Sermon on the

Mount). For instance, this question is behind the widespread debate on the ordination of women in light of 1 Corinthians 14:34–36, and 1 Timothy 2:8–15. Some argue that the use of creation and the fall in these passages anchors the command to silence (not to teach) in God's redemptive decrees and therefore it is meant for all ages. Others argue that the cultural background and the distance between the underlying principle (submission to husbands) and the command (not to teach) demonstrates a cultural rather than supracultural norm. The principle is that the supracultural content of Scripture is eternal/universal while cultural forms will apply the underlying principle differently depending upon the context.

Contextualization works with the results of the exegesis and cultural/supracultural delineation. It applies the biblical teaching to the receptor culture and its purpose is to allow the Word to encounter the world. At times it will conform to current culture and at other times it will confront modern man. In the latter sense Scripture will challenge and then transform that culture. For the evangelical, it is important to note, this is not a subjective decision. The authority of the application varies in direct proportion to its conformity to the meaning of the text. Furthermore, the level of authority lessens as one moves away from the Scripture itself. Interpretation, since it is finite, has less authority than the text, and contextualization, another step away from interpretation, has even less authority. Therefore, for the evangelical, the process of interpretation-contextualization must remain tied to the propositional content of God's revelation. Again, it is the dynamic or functional aspect of biblical authority.

9. *Hermeneutics: A Summary.* It is important to realize that the evangelical principles elucidated above are quite distinct from the lines of authority elucidated by Harrington and Burgess. The Reformation principle of *sola scriptura* and the Scottish Common Sense Realism of the last century have produced an extremely eclectic situation. There is not the type of uniformity stemming

from the Catholic principle of the magisterium. The sense of tradition is still true in evangelicalism, but it is under the surface of contemporary exposition and is restricted to denominational distinctives. This freedom has forced me to discuss constantly the different camps within evangelicalism on each of the issues above.

Above all, the importance of dialogue, or what I may call "community exegesis," must be stressed. It is through the interaction of the traditions that consensus is reached. This relates to the issue of separation discussed above and depends largely upon the evangelical willingness to dialogue with diverse traditions in order to arrive at "truth." For instance, while there is debate regarding the extent of inerrancy, there is consensus with respect to the propositional content of Scripture and the presence of both static and dynamic aspects of inspiration. The Bible deals with univocal truths expressed in analogical language, and so it is important to distinguish form from content. The exact details and significance of specific statements may differ, but the importance of the Bible for modern life is unilaterally accepted. As is the case with Catholicism, evangelicalism is tied more to the church than to the academy. The issues of our day set the agenda for much of scholarly research, and it is strongly argued that the Bible must relate to modern life if it is to be relevant. The steps of interpretation as explicated above are all necessary to this task.

CASE STUDY—EPHESIANS 2:1–10

While the question of the authorship of Ephesians is not crucial to the interpretation of this book, most evangelicals would affirm that Paul has written it.[25] It is part of the group called the prison or captivity epistles (Ephesians, Philippians, Colossians, Philemon). Many believe that it was a circular letter, sent to Asia Minor, since *en Ephesō* is missing in many ancient manuscripts and it has the tone in places of a treatise. Thematically it centers upon an exalted christology, that is, it presents the implications of the exalted Christ for the life of the church, particularly for its unity and mission. As such, Ephesians focuses upon two aspects, the above and the below, the already and the not yet. In this sense, the crucial phrase is "in the heavenlies," that realm where the exalted Christ operates (1:20), and where we presently reign with him (2:6). At the same time it is the sphere of cosmic warfare (6:12), and God's activity in redemption makes the church a living testimony to the cosmic forces of God's wisdom (3:10). Ephesians thus amalgamates the two spheres.

This tension is seen in chapters 1 to 3, which regulate God's activity in terms of his elect will (1:3–10) and the union of Jew and Gentile in the church (1:11–14). Ephesians 2:1–10 occurs at the juncture between the power of God operative in the church (1:19b–23) and the work of corporate salvation, centering upon the unity between Jew and Gentile, in 2:11–22. This paragraph describes the results of the divine salvific love upon those, Jew and Gentile alike, who were dead in sin.

The New International Version of the Bible, which was produced by an international group of Protestant scholars "committed to the full authority and complete trustworthiness of the Scriptures," translates Ephesians 2:1–10 as follows:

> [1]As for you, you were dead in your transgressions and sins, [2]in which you used to live when you followed the ways of this world and of the ruler of the kingdom of the air, the spirit who is now at work in those who are disobedient. [3]All of us also lived among them at one time, gratifying the cravings of our sinful nature and following its desires and thoughts. Like the rest, we were by nature objects of wrath. [4]But because of his great love for us, God, who is rich in mercy, [5]made us alive with Christ even when we were dead in transgressions—it is by grace you have been saved. [6]And God raised us up

with Christ and seated us with him in the heavenly realms in Christ Jesus, [7]in order that in the coming ages he might show the incomparable riches of his grace, expressed in his kindness to us in Christ Jesus. [8]For it is by grace you have been saved, through faith—and this not from yourselves, it is the gift of God—[9]not by works, so that no one can boast. [10]For we are God's workmanship, created in Christ Jesus to do good works, which God prepared in advance for us to do.

The evangelical would first attempt a detailed grammatical and structural analysis of the paragraph. This would yield two major points, the union of all in sin (vv. 1–3) and the overcoming power of God's gracious love (vv. 4–10). The "you"–"we" structure of vv. 1–3 is taken by some to parallel the Gentile ("you") and Jewish ("we") development of 1:11–14, but here the writer probably includes himself in both groups. The tone is clear: Sin is a result of influence from secular influences as well as hostile powers and results in rebellion, sensuality, and self-aggrandizement. The result is that all mankind is under the wrath of God.

Grammatically it is important to realize that the main verb for v. 1 does not appear until v. 5. As a result Paul keeps the reader in a state of tension as to the effects of "sin": Can it be overcome or not? The "then" and the "now" tension is clearly stressed, for Paul continues his accent upon the individual believer's privileges.[26] The realized side of salvation is central, and the basis is the sovereign act of God. It is not on the basis of personal merit or "work" but solely by divine "grace." The terminology utilized to describe this mercy shows how incomprehensible it is to man. No single term can describe it. The God who has procured salvation on our behalf is "rich in mercy" ("rich" is found six times in Ephesians, more often than in any other New Testament book, and in Ephesians–Colossians it is always used of God) and is characterized by "great love," a "grace" (twelve times

in Ephesians!) which is "immeasurably rich," and by "kindness."
All these reflect the Old Testament *hesed*, the "lovingkindness"
which is the basic relational attribute of God.

The sovereign control of God is clearly seen in the choice of
language. It is God who has "made us alive"; we were "dead in
transgressions" (v. 5). Salvation comes via "grace" (vv. 5b, 8a) and
is the "gift of God" (v. 8c); it is "not via works," which would lead
to "pride" (v. 9). It is clear that God alone distributes his salvific
power; redemption cannot be claimed on the basis of human
merit (for the Jew this specifically referred to legalistic right-
eousness; see Phil 3:9). In Ephesians 1–2, with a strong stress on
God's elective will as the basis of Christian blessings, Paul wants
the reader to understand perfectly that God, not man, is responsible for the basic privilege, salvation. It is clear in the context that
"saved" (v. 8) is employed more narrowly of "justification" rather
than broadly of the Christian life.

Yet the believer does have a part in the process. The "faith"-
response (v. 8) of the individual entails a complete openness or
surrender of the self to God's salvific action. It is clear here that
even this faith-response is not a work but itself is a "gift of God"
(see Phil 1:29); it is "not of ourselves" but is possible only because
of the enabling power of God.[27] At the same time it is important
to realize that Paul is not bypassing human choice, i.e., free will.
Of course there are many different formulations of this debate,
from Augustine versus Pelagius in the fifth century to the Cal-
vinist versus Arminian controversies of our own time. Whatever
one's perspective (and I confess that I am nearer to Arminius on
this issue), it is crucial here to preserve both sovereignty and free
will in the formula.

Moreover, I would stress the importance of community exegesis here. The interpreter must be in constant dialogue with
the past community of faith (the history of dogma) and the current community of faith (recent commentaries, etc.) on this point
as well as others.

The present and future results of this congruence between divine grace and human faith in salvation are also highlighted in 2:1–10. These are found in vv. 5–7, 10. First, the believer has been "made alive" or "raised up" (from spiritual death—v. 5a). For Paul the birth of faith is the hour of resurrection (see Rom 6:8; Gal 2:16, 20; Col 2:12; 3:1) and leads to "newness of life" (Rom 6:6; 2 Cor 5:17–20; Eph 4:22–24; Col 3:8–10). Second, God has "made (the believer) sit in the heavenlies with Christ," a remarkable passage in that it adds to Jesus' exaltation in 1:20 the Christian's exaltation here. This is the only place in the New Testament where Psalm 110:1, the most oft-quoted Old Testament passage in the New Testament, is applied to us. It is important to note the past tense, which indicates that this eschatological exaltation is not a future promise but a present reality, based undoubtedly on the Pauline metaphor of adoption. Due to God's gracious inclusion of us in his family, we are "joint-heirs" (Rom 8:15–17) and thus share Jesus' exalted status.

The final present blessing is found in v. 10, which relates our "creation" as God's "workmanship" in order that we might perform "good works." This is important as a clarification of the common belief that Paul and James are at odds on faith and works. A semantic mapwork of their use of terms indicates their basic agreement: A professed (but false) faith (James) which seeks works-righteousness (Paul) is useless (Paul and James); only a true faith (Paul) which leads to good works (James and Paul here in 2:10) is valid. The concept of faith put to work in acts of charity is central in the pastoral epistles, where "good works" appears eight times.

The future aspect is found in v. 7 and is important for the already-not yet tension in Ephesians (see above). While there is debate as to whether the "coming ages" means future generations of Christians or the eschaton, it is likely that no either–or response is possible. Both are probably in mind. The "immeasurable riches" manifested in his "kindness toward us" will be

CARL A. RUDISILL LIBRARY
LENOIR RHYNE COLLEGE

experienced by all future ages of the church and will be consummated in the second coming of Christ.

The contextualization (or "transfer value," to use Harrington's phrase above) of this passage is very direct for the evangelical. Meditation upon one's past state in sin is integral to the meaning of salvation. The three characteristics of vv. 2–3 (rebellion, sensuality, self-centeredness) describe the common dilemma of man, as demonstrated in recent sociological and psychological profiles of men and women in this modern post-industrial society. This, we would argue, is true of both secular man and those who now belong to the church.[28]

The distinction between conversion language and maintenance language posed by Harrington makes a great deal of sense here. Yet at the same time I doubt whether Paul would strongly emphasize the difference. The aorist (past) tenses of the verbs ("made alive," "raised up," "made to sit") must be seen in the light of the perfect periphrastic "have been saved," which stresses the present condition. Paul actually is stressing the present Christian situation of resurrection life which has resulted from the past conversion. Once again, it is not an either–or. For this reason, the dynamic power, the exalted status and the concomitant demand for good works are eminently applicable. Finally, the evangelical endorses the necessity of conversion language for our day. The depravity of man, the salvific sacrifice of Christ, and the indispensability of faith-decision are at the heart of the revivalist spirit so endemic to the movement.

SUMMARY

Evangelicals have always made a "high" view of biblical authority a basic tenet of their faith. In spite of the widespread debate today over the exact formulation of such issues as "inerrancy," evangelicals consistently stress that Scripture alone must dictate our faith. While there is cognizance of the complex nature of the interpretive task and the factor of pre-understanding as shaping that interpretation, there is unanimity that the intention of the author is both a possible goal and a necessary element in determining the meaning of the Bible in our day. At the same time, the relevant significance of Scripture is also stressed, and the interdependence between exegesis, biblical theology, historical theology, systematic theology, and contextualization forms the core of evangelical hermeneutics.

The grammatical-historical method predominates. The tools of textual and source criticism, syntactical (grammar) and semantic (word) study, and form, redaction, and narrative criticisms, are all subordinate to the task of elucidating the text. After several decades of isolation, there is a growing desire once again to engage in dialogue with other traditions, and indeed this book is an important part of that movement. An "evangelical" reading of Ephesians 2:1–10 stresses the Pauline origin of the teaching and its connection with Romans 1–8 and related texts. The progress of the passage fits the dilemma of modern humanity, locked in sin and needing to apply the salvific grace of God and the sacrifice of Christ in a conversion experience. Divine grace and human faith meet in the supreme gift of faith-decision. This unlocks God's workmanship inherent in man/woman, leading to the "good works" which characterize the presence of God in the community.

NOTES

1. George B. Marsden, *Fundamentalism and American Culture: The Shaping of Twentieth Century Evangelicalism, 1870–1925* (New York: Oxford University Press, 1980) 113 (cf. 111–15), quote from A.A. Hodge and B.B. Warfield, "Inspiration," *The Presbyterian Review II* (April 1881) 234. See also Ernest Sandeen, *The Roots of Fundamentalism* (Chicago: University of Chicago

Press, 1970) 103–31, and Jack Rogers and Donald McKim, *The Authority and Interpretation of the Bible: An Historical Approach* (New York: Harper and Row, 1979) 265–347.

2. John Woodbridge, *Biblical Authority: A Critique of the Rogers/McKim Proposal* (Grand Rapids: Zondervan, 1982) 219 (n. 88).

3. Timothy P. Weber, "The Two-Edged Sword: The Fundamentalist Use of the Bible," *The Bible in America: Essays in Cultural History,* ed. Nathan O. Hatch and Mark A. Noll (New York: Oxford University Press, 1982) 109 (cf. 102–10).

4. See Louis Gasper, *The Fundamentalist Movement, 1930–1956* (Grand Rapids: Baker, 1981) 1–20 ("The Fundamentalist Heritage"), and Norman F. Furniss, *The Fundamentalist Controversy, 1918–1931* (New Haven: Yale University Press, 1954) 117–88.

5. For reactions within the Arminian, Holiness, and Pentecostal sectors, see Vinson Tyson, "Theological Boundaries: The Arminian Tradition," *The Evangelicals,* ed. David F. Wells and John D. Woodbridge (Grand Rapids: Baker, 1975) 38–57.

6. George Marsden, "From Fundamentalism to Evangelicalism: A Historical Analysis," *The Evangelicals,* ed. Wells and Woodbridge, 147, calls the period from 1926 to the 1940s a stage of "withdrawal and regrouping," during which time sectarianism predominated and both separatism and millenarianism became tests of orthodoxy. This, however, was true only in the mainstream of fundamentalism. On the edges, for instance among many reformed Wesleyan and Anabaptist groups, this did not hold true.

7. See Joel Carpenter, "Fundamentalist Institutions and the Rise of Evangelical Protestantism, 1929–1942," *Church History* 49 (1980) 73–75. He argues that the four basic areas of fundamentalist activity (education, Bible conferences, radio broadcasting and foreign missions) demonstrated "a growing, dynamic movement." There was no "American Religious Depression" in

the 1930s but rather a shift of emphasis from polemics to evangelism.

8. See Jerry Falwell, *The Fundamentalist Phenomenon: The Resurgence of Conservative Christianity* (Garden City, N.Y.: Doubleday, 1981).

9. Harold Lindsell, *Battle for the Bible* (Grand Rapids: Zondervan Publishing House, 1976), and *The Bible in the Balance* (Grand Rapids: Zondervan Publishing House, 1979).

10. J. Robertson McQuilkin, *Understanding and Applying the Bible* (Chicago: Moody Press, 1983) 10. See also J.I. Packer, "Infallible Scripture and the Role of Hermeneutics," *Scripture and Truth,* ed. D.A. Carson and John D. Woodbridge (Grand Rapids: Zondervan, 1983) 325–56, who speaks of "the centrality of hermeneutics today" (325–27).

11. Walter Kaiser, *Toward an Exegetical Theology* (Grand Rapids: Baker Book House, 1981) 82. He clarifies this by arguing that a misuse of the "analogy of faith," in which a future passage is utilized to interpret a previous one, is equally wrong.

12. For good discussions of this, see Charles M. Wood, *The Formation of Christian Understanding: An Essay in Theological Hermeneutics* (Philadelphia: Westminster, 1981), and David H. Kelsey, *The Uses of Scripture in Recent Theology* (Philadelphia: Fortress Press, 1975). Kelsey has a "functional" view of authority which sees Scripture as providing "patterns" rather than concepts.

13. E.D. Hirsch, *Validity in Interpretation* (New Haven: Yale University Press, 1967) 72–88. For a slightly different proposal, centering on the text rather than the author, see P.D. Juhl, *Interpretation: An Essay in the Philosophy of Literary Criticism* (Princeton: Princeton University Press, 1980) 12–15. Two who follow closely this argument are Walter Kaiser, "The Single Intent of Scripture," *Evangelical Roots,* ed. Kenneth Kantzer (Nashville: Thomas Nelson, 1978), and Elliott Johnson, *Hermeneutics* (Grand Rapids: Zondervan, forthcoming).

14. Moises Silva, *Biblical Words and Their Meaning: An Introduction to Lexical Semantics* (Grand Rapids: Zondervan, 1983) 148.

15. Paul Achtemeier, *The Inspiration of Scripture: Problems and Proposals* (Philadelphia: Westminster, 1980) 57–75.

16. D.A. Carson, "Unity and Diversity in the New Testament: The Possibility of Systematic Theology," *Scripture and Truth*, ed. Carson and Woodbridge, 90–93 (cf. 139–41).

17. Wayne A. Grudem, "Scripture's Self-Attestation and the Problem of Formulating a Doctrine of Scripture," *Scripture and Truth*, 49 (cf. 19–59).

18. A.C. Thiselton, *The Two Horizons: New Testament Hermeneutics and Philosophical Description* (Grand Rapids: Eerdmans, 1980) 437 (cf. 432–38).

19. Robert Gundry, *Matthew: A Commentary on His Literary and Theological Art* (Grand Rapids: Eerdmans, 1981). See my review article in *TSF Bulletin*, 6/4 (March–April 1983) 14–16, which relates the comments of the symposia on his work at ETS and AAR in December 1982.

20. See the discussion in Weber, "The Two-Edged Sword," *The Bible in America*, 111–14. Weber describes this synthetic method in this way: "Once the whole was in hand, one could turn one's attention to a more detailed study of its component parts . . ." (112–13).

21. See Robert H. Stein, *An Introduction to the Parables of Jesus* (Philadelphia: Westminster, 1981).

22. For evangelical responses, see my "The Evangelical and *Traditionsgeschichte*," *Journal of the Evangelical Theological Society* 21/2 (1978) 117–30, and R.H. Stein, "The 'Criteria' for Authenticity," *Gospel Perspectives I*, ed. R.T. France and David Wenham (Sheffield: JSOT Press, 1980) 225–63.

23. See Gerhard Maier, *The End of the Historical-Critical Method* (St. Louis: Concordia, 1977), and Gerhard Hasel, *Understanding the Living Word of God* (Mountain View, Cal.: Pacific Press, 1980).

24. See Edwin Yamauchi, *The Stones and the Scriptures* (Philadelphia: Lippincott, 1972) 146–57.

25. See A. van Roon, *The Authenticity of Ephesians* (Leiden: Brill, 1974). For further data, see Andrew Lincoln's review article in *Westminster Theological Journal* 40 (1977–78) 172–75.

26. For the corporate versus individual stress in Ephesians 1–2, see C.L. Mitton, *Ephesians* (New Century Bible; Greenwood, S.C.: Attic Press, 1976) 79–80. While he overdoes the individualistic aspect somewhat, he is basically correct that Paul here is looking at the individual within the Church.

27. See the fine discussion of this point in Markus Barth, *Ephesians* (Anchor Bible; Garden City, N.Y.: Doubleday, 1974) 224–25. He points to the conjunction here of God's (and Christ's) faithfulness with our faith.

28. Here the application depends upon one's view of the sacrament of baptism. Most evangelicals, even from a strongly sacramental position, would argue that a later faith-decision parallel to that in this passage must occur.

RECOMMENDED READINGS

D. A. Carson and John Woodbridge (eds.), *Scripture and Truth* (Grand Rapids: Zondervan, 1983). A series of essays centering upon the importance of inerrancy and a propositional approach to Scripture.

Gordon Fee and Douglas Stuart, *How To Read the Bible for All Its Worth* (Philadelphia: Westminster, 1982). An excellent general discussion on the proper approach to specific genres, e.g. poetry, wisdom, gospels, Acts.

Nathan O. Hatch and Mark A. Noll (eds.), *The Bible in America: Essays in Cultural History* (New York: Oxford University Press, 1982). A series of essays tracing the progress of interpretation in various traditions in American Christianity.

George B. Marsden, *Fundamentalism and American Culture: The Shaping of Twentieth Century Evangelicalism 1870–1925* (New York: Oxford University Press, 1980). A major work on the factors which led to the fundamentalist/evangelical movement.

I. Howard Marshall (ed.), *New Testament Interpretation: Essays on Principles and Methods* (Grand Rapids: Eerdmans, 1977). Essays tracing various schools and issues in the field of hermeneutics, demonstrating the many differences in the approaches of evangelicals as they interact with diverse critical issues.

Roger R. Nicole and J. Ramsey Michaels (eds.), *Inerrancy and Common Sense* (Grand Rapids: Baker, 1980). Essays tracing various aspects, both academic and practical, on the issue of biblical authority. More than other works on inerrancy, this demonstrates the various evangelical approaches.

Jack Rogers and Donald McKim, *Authority and Interpretation of the Bible* (New York: Harper and Row, 1979). An attempt to show that a more dynamic model of biblical authority existed from the patristic period until the Princetonians of the last century.

Moises Silva, *Biblical Words and Their Meaning: An Introduction to Lexical Semantics* (Grand Rapids: Zondervan, 1983). Not only a study of the methods of lexical study but also an illustration of the implications of a propositional approach to Scripture.

Anthony C. Thiselton, *The Two Horizons: New Testament Hermeneutics and Philosophical Description* (Grand Rapids: Eerdmans, 1980). A major discussion of the hermeneutical problem of the past (what it meant) and present (what it means) problem in interpretation theory, using the approaches of Heidegger, Bultmann, and Gadamer as the control.

John D. Woodbridge, *Biblical Authority: A Critique of the Rogers/McKim Proposal* (Grand Rapids: Zondervan, 1982). Argues contra Rogers and McKim (above) that the Church down through the ages held a view of propositional authority or total infallibility.

Joseph A. Burgess

Lutheran Interpretation of Scripture

What proof do you have? What evidence do you have? With such questions you are raising the problem of authority. And ultimately any discussion of the problem of authority leads to the question of final authority. What is your final authority? Archimedes said that if you would give him a place to stand on, he could move the world. Christians will state that their final authority is God, Christ, the Holy Spirit, or the Bible. All Christians hold *sola scriptura* to be the final authority, even though *sola scriptura* may be modified by words such as "and Christ," "and tradition," "and experience," or "and reason."

Sola scriptura is the claim, yet what this claim means needs to be sorted out. One cartoon shows a package descending from the sky suspended from a parachute. The label on the package says "Holy Bible." Another cartoon has God sitting on a cloud and speaking through a megaphone; four tubes descend from the megaphone to earth, where Matthew, Mark, Luke, and John are sitting at desks writing down what they hear. We smile and dismiss such cartoons as caricatures. But at the opening lecture on the Bible at a Lutheran seminary the teacher picked up a Bible, placed it on the floor, and actually stood on the Bible for several moments. He intended to dramatize the fact that he took his stand on the Bible. The students were horrified, for to them it was sacrilegious to use the Bible like this. After all, the Bible is a "holy" book, sometimes even venerated in worship. Somehow this paper and ink is different from all other paper and ink. Or is it? Has a concept of material holiness crept in from the Old Testament, where certain objects may not be touched or even looked at because they are holy (see Num 4:15, 19–20; 1 Chr 13:9–10)? Here authority has been understood as raw power. Only God, of course, has raw power in the ultimate sense, for he is omnipotent and no one can compete with his power.

At the other extreme *sola scriptura* means no more than that the Bible is an important document but one among many important documents. There is no word from the Lord, from outside of myself. Ultimately I have to depend on myself, my reason, my feelings, my experience, or my conscience. At this point the uniqueness of the Bible is lost because of historical criticism. Historical criticism, to be sure, must be defined. First of all, what is "historical"? Second, what is "criticism"? If historical means that there is no word from God, that the only authority I have is my experience, then I am caught in relativism, for reason, feelings, experience, and even conscience vary in my own life and in the course of history. If criticism means that I am the judge of all that is or is not, then I have made myself the final authority for all things and have fallen into relativism. According to this, the most virulent definition of historical criticism, the Bible has authority only to the extent that I give it authority.

It is important to note that other definitions of historical criticism are possible and even appropriate. What is needed at this point is that you and I react to the assertion that there is no word from the Lord, that the Bible is not unique, that I am the final authority. We know that we are more uncomfortable with this assertion than the other extreme. Lutherans take the Bible very seriously, holding that it is the "only rule and norm according to which all doctrines and teachers alike must be appraised and judged" (*Formula of Concord,* Epitome, 1). Lutherans differ, one must quickly interject, on how to apply this principle; some Lutherans even hold a view of the Bible which looks very much like fundamentalism, although the vast majority do not belong in this camp. But there can be no doubt about the centrality of *sola scriptura* in the Lutheran tradition.

How Is the Bible Different?

Lutherans differ on how the Bible is different even while agreeing that the Bible is the sole authority for all proclamation, teaching, and life in the church. No official Lutheran teaching on the inspiration of the Bible exists, although some have tried to derive a doctrine of inspiration from the Lutheran Confessions. There is no official Lutheran list of the books of the Bible, and for that reason the canon of Scripture is in principle open for Lutherans; in actual fact Lutherans operate with the same basic canon that most Protestants use, and it would be false to imply that Lutherans have had any desire to add to the canon.

A. IS THE BIBLE DIFFERENT BECAUSE IT IS INSPIRED?

Lutherans take the Bible very seriously because it is the only source we have for God's word. But why only the Bible? What makes it different? Since the difference is not in the paper and ink and since the same words and sequences of words are used as in other literature, what possible claim can be made that the Bible is different? As is well known, the claim is that the Bible was written by the inspiration of the Holy Spirit and therefore the Bible is unlike all other books. Other religions also claim that their holy books are inspired, but Christians claim that the Bible is inspired by the Spirit of the one true God.

Every Christian holds that the Bible is inspired. The question is: "How?" Various theories of inspiration exist, and each claims to describe the method the Holy Spirit used. No theory denies the Holy Spirit. For example, because Christians hold that everyone received the Holy Spirit through baptism, some would hold that the Holy Spirit continues to inspire the writings done by Christians. At the other extreme are those claiming that God gave the words, inspired someone to write, and that person simply held the pen.

There is no one biblical theory of inspiration, although the Bible contains several theories of inspiration. Thousands of passages state "the Lord said," "thus says the Lord," "the Lord spoke," "the Lord spoke to," and the like. The difficulty is that what is meant is not obvious. Was the Lord speaking in such a way that everyone standing about heard? Or was the Lord speaking in such a way that the prophet alone heard, and in this case were sounds heard or were ideas registered? If ideas, were they filtered through the prophet's mind or were they ideas the prophet could write down without being altered by the prophet's historical context? In all probablity most of the writers of the Bible did not agonize over such questions but simply assumed that what they said and wrote was inspired by God. At times, to be sure, when it was a question of true or false prophecy and teaching, they did agonize and even provided certain kinds of answers (see Dt 13:1–5; 1 Kgs 22:28; Gal 1:6–9).

In the history of the first giving of the ten commandments on Mount Sinai the writer describes how Moses wrote down the words of the Lord, yet in the same chapter the Lord says he has done the writing (Ex 24:4, 12). In the history of the second giving of the ten commandments the Lord writes on the two tables of stone, yet Moses later in the chapter is the one who wrote on the two tables (Ex 34:1, 28). How does one sort out the theory of inspiration in these passages? Only with great difficulty can a theory be proposed unless one resorts to complex explanations or unless editorial interference is suggested. In 2 Kings 3:15 the prophet asks for a minstrel to be brought; when the minstrel played, the prophet was inspired. This fits in with the mantic theory of inspiration in the ancient world. The musician was possessed and in this way inspired by the spirit. The prophet in turn could be inspired through the musician (1 Chr 25:1). In Zechariah 13:4–6 lacerations have been used by the false prophets to produce prophetic ecstasy, but the practice is found in the official religious life as well (Jer 41:5; 1 Kgs 18:28–29).

The most famous New Testament passage dealing with inspiration is 2 Timothy 3:16: "All scripture is inspired," according to the translation found in the King James Version. But the New English Bible translates: "Every inspired scripture has its use." This is at least a very acceptable version of the Greek text and brings out the fact that "scripture" in this context means the Old Testament. When one recalls the radical freedom with which New Testament writers make use of the Old Testament, one must be cautious about any theory of inspiration which would imply that the text was thought to be so holy that it must not be interpreted except in a very literal fashion. The adjective translated as "inspired" simply means "God-breathed," and no particular theory of inspiration is implied by the word. In 2 Peter 1:21 prophecy is not from human efforts, for prophets are those "moved by the Holy Spirit." Obviously this means that prophets are those guided by the Holy Spirit, but in what way and to what extent is not defined.

Paul distinguishes between God's words and his own words (1 Cor 7:6, 10, 12, 25, 40), but he does not describe how this is done or what makes God's words different. What does Paul mean when he writes: "We impart this in words not taught by human wisdom but taught by the Spirit" (1 Cor 2:13)? Who is the "we" in this passage? Is it Paul, or is it an editorial "we," or is it all true Christians? Furthermore, what "words" are meant here? Are these Paul's words in this letter, or the words he uses in preaching, or is it the words used by true Christians when they testify? Similar questions arise with a phrase like "in the Spirit" (Mt 22:42; Rev 1:10) and the assertion that the Holy Spirit "will teach you all things and bring to your remembrance all that I have said to you" (Jn 14:26). How does the Holy Spirit do this, and to what extent? The conclusion from looking at the Bible on inspiration is that since no monolithic theory of inspiration is found in the Bible, the approach to the Bible should be doxological, that is, we can only approach the Bible with praise and thanksgiving because it bursts every category and theory we might have.

A brief survey of the theories of inspiration in church history shows how theories developed according to the historical context. Inspiration in the Old Testament usually meant that the personality of the writer was not overpowered by the spirit but rather interacted with the spirit. Christianity, however, came from the strand of Judaism called Hellenistic Judaism, which had appropriated the Hellenistic idea that the inspired writer has been used by God the way a musician uses a lyre or a flute. This mantic view of inspiration can be found in Philo, Josephus, 4 Ezra, and the Talmud. Christians used the analogy of the lyre or flute up to and including Irenaeus, but because of the rise of Montanism, which also claimed that its prophets had been mantically inspired, the mantic theory of inspiration came to be a sign of false prophecy. The mantic theory continued to be used as an apologetic device in battles against heresy, but during the Middle Ages for the most part a theory of inspiration was not emphasized because the tradition of the church was the basis for authority.

The change at the time of the Reformation was not a new or renewed theory of inspiration. Luther took the Bible very seriously, as did others before him, yet he also could use the Bible very critically, as is well known, for example, from his statements about the epistle of James as an "epistle of straw." The Lutheran *Book of Concord* did not prescribe any formal doctrine of inspira-

tion for Lutherans. In the polemics of the second generation of
the Reformation, however, mantic views of inspiration returned,
for example, in Flacius Illyricus, who held that even the Hebrew
vowels are inspired. During the so-called period of Orthodoxy in
the seventeenth century, polemic fronts hardened and mantic
views of inspiration became very important, notably in Gerhard,
Calov, and Quenstedt among the Lutherans and Voetius, "covenant" theology, and the *Formula Consensus Helvetica* of 1675
among the Reformed.

The synthesis which Orthodoxy tried to establish failed, for
the modern world was breaking through. Not only had voyages
of discovery found that there are strong religions elsewhere in
the world and Copernicus shown that human beings are not the
center of the universe, but the Age of Reason culminating in
Kant's philosophy raised questions about the place of Christianity in the total scheme of life. The French Revolution in 1789
challenged traditional political, social, and religious authority. In
the nineteenth century Darwin produced a theory of evolution,
questioning the uniqueness of human beings. Toward the end of
that century Freud developed models of the human mind which
challenged traditional views of human consciousness and drives.
In this century Einstein's theory of relativity, Heisenberg's principle of indeterminacy, nuclear weapons, landing on the moon,
and genetic engineering, to name but a few in a long list, have
been further shocks to traditional authorities and beliefs.

Traditionalists, faced with what they perceived as relativism,
scientism, historicism, secularism, and atheism, reached for traditional weapons. Roman Catholics worked out and then finally
in 1870 defined papal primacy and infallibility. Anglicans produced the Oxford Movement. In the nineteenth century some
Lutherans, such as Vilmar and Stahl, emphasized the Lutheran
Confessions and a high view of the minister's authority. But the
mantic theory of inspiration also was a major weapon that Lutheran traditionalists made use of as they defended what they

perceived as the true faith under attack by error. Other Lutherans adopted Reformed "covenant" theology ("salvation history"), according to which revelation takes place through the
historical events themselves and therefore attacks made on the
written text cannot affect the "inspired" events; already Bengel
in the eighteenth century was famous for following this line of
thought, and it continued in the nineteenth century in such theologians as von Hofmann, Rothe, and Mencken. A different tack
was taken by Schleiermacher, who held that the Holy Spirit is
identical with the Spirit in the church; for this reason the Spirit
which guided the apostles when they wrote is not essentially different from the Spirit which guides each Christian today. The
apostles, to be sure, would have a stronger measure of the Spirit
because they were closer to Christ's Spirit.

Variations on these theories of inspiration continue today;
no one theory dominates. All would contend in some way that the
Bible is both human and divine, but whether this would be by
analogy with Christ's humanity and divinity, an analogy already
suggested by Chrysostom in the early church, would be a matter
of dispute because not all would agree that since Christ's humanity is without sin, therefore the Bible must be without error. Does
the fact that Jesus lived without sin mean that while walking he
could not stub his toe on a rock?

B. IS THE BIBLE DIFFERENT BECAUSE IT IS CANON?

The problem of the Bible as canon is the unexamined ecumenical problem, a land mine waiting to explode. The general
question of the relationship between the Bible and tradition, to
be sure, has been discussed, as for example in 1963 at the world
conference of Faith and Order of the World Council of
Churches. But in spite of basic differences that exist among
churches, ecumenical dialogues have simply assumed that a consensus exists on the nature and extent of the canon. At stake is

not simply the fact that some hold the apocrypha to be canonical and others do not. Rather, the nature of the Bible itself is decisive for all other theological questions. It can be said that Lutherans hold to the fact but not the extent of the canon because Lutherans are not tied to a specific list of books in the Bible. Yet what does it mean to hold to the fact of the canon? Within the Bible itself the word is used (Gal 6:16; see Rom 6:17), but how "canon" applies to the Bible is of course not spelled out.

The problems are complex. How do we deal with the fact that 1 Enoch 1:9 is quoted as prophecy in Jude 14–15? In 1 Corinthians 2:9, using the technical formula "it is written," which indicates authoritative Scripture, Paul cites a passage not in the Old Testament. 1 Clement, written A.D. 95–96, the letters of Ignatius, written about A.D. 110, and the Didache, also written about A.D. 110, are not included in the New Testament canon, but 1 and 2 Timothy and Titus, written during the same period, are included. 1 Clement and the Didache were, after all, in some early lists and collections. What if the lost letter to the Laodiceans (Col 4:16) were found? Would we include it in the canon, and, if so, how would we decide? Would anything except an ecumenical council be able to make such a decision?

Lest we fall into the mistake of simply asserting that the canon is the canon is the canon and therefore the nature of the canon is self-evident, it is important to become aware of the various attempts in church history to define the canon.

1. What is canonical is determined by orthodox content. Where the Spirit of Christ is, there is the canon. But where is the Spirit? Where do we find orthodox content? The difficulty with this attempt is that it is precisely the canon which is supposed to define where the Spirit is and what is orthodox. Furthermore, in the early church, orthodoxy and heresy were not so easy to discern. In that early period lines were fluid. Only after long debate and struggle did orthodoxy emerge and heresy become evident.

2. What is canonical is apostolic. But who are apostles according to the New Testament? Luke thinks of twelve apostles, the eleven plus Matthias (Acts 1:26), plus two, Paul and Barnabas (Acts 14:4, 14). In Romans 16:7 Paul writes of Andronicus and Junias who were apostles before him, in Philippians 2:25 Epaphroditus is called an apostle, and in 2 Corinthians 8:24 apostles are simply those who are missionaries. The New Testament books by Mark, Luke, and Jude are clearly not written by apostles, and if the claim is made that these men were closely associated with apostles, then already the understanding of apostolicity has been greatly widened. Very early questions were raised about the Pauline authorship of Hebrews; in spite of being associated with "John," the Book of Revelation was the last book accepted into the canon because its form and content did not match other Johannine literature and because it seemed to lend support to Montanism.

3. What is canonical is early or the earliest. To go back to the sources is not only an appeal to tradition, in this case the early or earliest tradition, but also an appeal to the humanistic principle that one must go back to the sources. What comes from the early church establishes the canon, or what belongs to the era of salvation history establishes the canon. Yet, as is well known, not all the writings from the early tradition have been included in the canon. Even if the earliest writings are more likely to be a more accurate reflection of what was said and done, some were not selected for the canon. The early church struggled with this problem, for some early writings, like Barnabas, were included and then rejected, while others, like Revelation, were rejected and finally included.

4. What is canonical is what the church establishes as canonical. If this were the case, the church would be more authoritative than the Bible. Some would take this point of view. As a matter of fact, however, formal recognition of the canon by the

church took place rather later in the process. The first time that all twenty-seven books in the New Testament were listed was by Athanasius in his Easter letter in A.D. 367. The first formal recognition by the church of this list of books came from a local council at Hippo in A.D. 393; another local council followed suit at Carthage in A.D. 397. Innocent I in A.D. 405 cited this same list. In some parts of the Orthodox church the Book of Revelation was not accepted until the tenth century. At Florence in A.D. 1442 the Roman Catholic church for the first time formally defined the extent of the biblical canon. As already noted, Lutherans have not formally defined the extent of the canon. The Bible of the Nestorian church in Syria, the Peshitta, has only twenty-two books in the New Testament, while the Bible of the Ethiopian church has thirty-one books in its New Testament canon.

Already in the second century the sayings of Jesus and letters of Paul had canonical authority, but it took centuries for the canon of the New Testament as we now know it to be established. Even the gospel of John was not fully accepted until the end of the second century because it was suspected by some to have gnostic tendencies. If the claim is made that the church establishes the canon, the question must be asked: Which church and at what point in history? Most important of all, however, is that those making this claim understand the church to be more authoritative than the Bible.

5. What is canonical is what has been used as canonical. The canon has simply developed; certain books have been used, and for this reason they have formed the canon. The difficulty with this attempt to explain the canon is that there has been a great deal of variety. At one point Hermas, 2 Clement, and the Apocalypse of Peter were included. Why were the letters of Ignatius not used as canonical letters? To claim that usage makes a book canonical does not explain why certain books were used and others not used.

6. What is canonical is what is found in the early creeds. For example, 1 Corinthians 8:6 and 15:3–5 are creeds or fragments of creeds used in the early church. According to this viewpoint such creeds are canonical; they are the final authorities for the Christian faith. Thus a certain pattern of preaching developed and became normative, a pattern of authenticity. Later, in the second century, Papias would claim unique authority for the sayings of Jesus. About this time the Roman creed also played a role in defining the Christian faith.

But from all the creeds and fragments of creeds, where does one find "the" creed, "the" pattern which is normative? In addition, one must ask if this attempt to establish the canon does not make the twenty-seven books of the New Testament subordinate to the creed.

7. What is canonical is what the internal testimony of the Holy Spirit shows is canonical. A woman told of the great spiritual blessing she received from the word "selah" in the psalms. Yet scholars are not certain of the meaning of "selah"; it probably is some sort of direction to the conductor for the music. Does not this attempt to establish the nature of the canon ultimately mean that my internal experience becomes the final authority? How is one to distinguish between the spirits (1 Jn 4:1)?

8. What is canonical is the canon within the canon. The canon within the canon is not the canon in a wooden sense. In other words, the canon within the canon is not a certain passage from the Bible, such as John 3:16, or a certain author, such as Paul or John or Matthew, or a certain book, such as Revelation. The canon within the canon is that which is used to deal with difficulties found within the Bible. The Bible contains such difficulties when it is taken literally. As a consequence each tradition uses some kind of hermeneutics to sort out these difficulties. Each tradition has a theological approach to the Bible, an approach often described as the "hermeneutics of the gospel"; what is meant is that by this process the central truth of the Bible can

be discerned and kept intact. In a sense the historical canon and theological canon stand in tension. The canon within the canon is not an authority by itself, separate from the gospel, the theological canon, and the canon within the canon is not an authority separate from the book called the Bible, the historical canon. Nevertheless, the hermeneutics of the gospel is that which determines the central truth called the gospel, and each Christian tradition has its own "hermeneutics of the gospel," its canon within the canon. A Lutheran "hermeneutics of the gospel" will be described later in this chapter.

BASIC QUESTIONS AND PRESUPPOSITIONS

Christ is the answer. What is the question? The question might be: How does one decide that Christ is the answer? Or the question might be: What does it mean that Christ is the answer? Then all sorts of questions and presuppositions come into play. The point is that although all agree that Christ is the answer, not all agree on what this means. Nor does it help to claim to hold to Scripture as absolutely inerrant and infallible in every detail or to claim to use a method of interpreting Scripture that is literal and "historical-grammatical" instead of "historical-critical," for there is clearly no unanimity among those claiming to hold such positions.

But there is no unanimity among those claiming to use the historical-critical method either. Therefore some other criterion will have to be found for deciding whether the historical-critical method is acceptable for those holding to Christ as the answer. Those who attack the historical-critical method apply certain tests, and these tests are really the presuppositions of those opposing the historical-critical method.

A. THE PRESUPPOSITION
OF THE UNITY OF SCRIPTURE

The historical-critical method asks: "What happened?" What it discovers is not only that the Bible was written over many hundreds of years and in many different literary forms but also that the Bible contains a great variety of ideas, some of which at least appear to oppose each other. A famous example is the story of King David's census; in 2 Samuel 24:1 it is reported that the Lord incited David to take the census, whereas in 1 Chronicles 21:1 it says that Satan incited David to number Israel. Historical critics unravel the difficulty in these verses by noting that they were written by different authors at different times with different theologies.

Opponents of historical criticism presuppose the unity of Scripture. Is this a unity such as Christians posit for the Trinity, a unity which is finally a mystery? Or is this a unity which excludes contradictions, a unity built on logic, so that even if items stand in contradiction, a contradiction cannot exist because the presupposition of unity does not allow for contradiction? In that case the reader is expected to suspend judgment, to oppose his intellect, because of the supreme authority of the presupposition of unity. Most of the time, to be sure, the unity of Scripture is defended by means of an overarching concept such as the Word, or the covenant, or salvation history, or God's plan, or God's kingly rule, or God's grace.

The rejoinder by the historical critics is simple: How are difficulties solved by refusing to deal with them? More importantly, is it not in fact true that instead of working on the basis of the unity of Scripture, each stream of Christian tradition uses its own theological approach, its own canon within the canon, to sort out and solve the difficulties in Scripture?

B. THE PRESUPPOSITION THAT REASON IS TO BE SUBORDINATE TO SCRIPTURE

The basis for this presupposition is often 2 Corinthians 10:5: "We destroy arguments and every proud obstacle to the knowledge of God, and take every thought captive to obey Christ" (see 1 Cor 1:18–25). At first glance no one would fault this argument. Reason is not God, and reason cannot be superior to Scripture. Scripture tells us who we are and who God is, not reason. Reason can at best play a servant role, as a tool which helps us understand more fully what Scripture means.

The question, of course, is whether reason for historical critics is necessarily made superior to Scripture or whether historical critics do not also use reason as a tool. During the French Revolution, to be sure, reason was made into a goddess, and no doubt individuals have made reason superior to revelation. But for the vast majority historical criticism is a method, not a philosophy. In order to penetrate more deeply into the meaning of Scripture, it is necessary to think. Thinking always includes the use of the principle of analogy, for how else is it possible to comprehend at all? Surely no one would claim that Scripture must in princple be irrational or incomprehensible? Nor did Paul in 1 Corinthians 1:18–25 and 2 Corinthians 10:5 intend to reject thinking or trying to comprehend Scripture with the use of modern historical tools. Furthermore modern thinkers are well aware of the fact that reason itself is part of history and subject to change.

C. THE PRESUPPOSITION THAT MIRACLES HAPPEN

But what is a miracle? The common understanding among those raising this question is that miracles are evidence or proof. By this they understand creation to be run by natural laws, like a clock; a miracle is that which breaks into such a world and in doing so provides proof that God has intervened. Some would also point out that the modern scientific view of the world as an open system allows for miracles, and others would also claim that through God's sustaining work everything is miracle. As a result the Christian faith can be defended as truth because there is evidence to back up the faith; few, to be sure, would deny that faith is also needed, but the important thing is that the proofs are there for all who are willing to see. And the proofs are there because the Bible records such miracles and intends them to be evidence and proof.

Those using the historical-critical method do not reject "miracles" in the sense defined above, for as defined above "miracles" stand outside of history and the historian can only state "I don't know." But the historian is able to ask the question whether the Bible intended "miracle" to be understood in the sense defined above. Not everyone who observed a miracle was convinced, and some said that Jesus did miracles by the power of Beelzebul (Mk 3:22). Thus it was well known that miracles were done by those who were not Christians. The gospel of John has a very complex understanding of "signs" or "miracles" (see 2:23–25; 3:2; 6:26; 10:19–21; 11:45–48; 20:29–31). Paul indicates that demanding "signs" is one way the Jews show their unbelief, for Christians hold to the stumbling-block of Christ crucified (1 Cor 1:22; see 2 Cor 12:9–13). The historian is also aware of the fact that literary forms sometimes give the reader a clue to the intent of a miracle story. The important point, however, is that the historian does not try to deny or destroy what the Bible describes; rather, the historical critic helps us understand the text and in fact helps us focus on Jesus Christ alone and him crucified (see 1 Cor 2:2).

D. THE PRESUPPOSITION OF FACTICITY

It is a fact that the modern mind often assumes that "facts" exist. What is meant is that a certain kind of information is demonstrable, directly accessible to the five senses, and available to all human beings. A popular view of science is that science is able to produce facts. Sometimes it is assumed that history also is able to produce facts and that the Bible, a book of history, is full of facts which Christians are to believe in. Historical criticism, in turn, is thought by some to be very destructive because it seems to question some of the facts in the Bible.

The trouble with "facts" is that truly modern science no longer claims to produce facts but rather statistical averages. And modern historical study no longer claims to produce facts but rather a record of interpretations and ideas. Even the person on the street knows that an accident at the crossroads will be interpreted differently by different witnesses. And even the person on the street knows that people in other times and cultures perceived and thought differently.

On the other hand, the person on the street still thinks the words have a specific meaning, a meaning which can be established by means of a dictionary after determining the context. What people do not realize is that dictionaries are history books, which is quickly perceived when someone looks into the Oxford English Dictionary, for example. Grammar is the same kind of problem. Most suppose that grammar is exact, that "correct" usage can be established. Some think that with a "historical-grammatical" method it is possible to avoid the perils of the historical-critical method. Yet grammar too is historical and depends on the philosophies of language operative at a specific time. In general it can be said that theologians need to bring the symbolic nature of words and "facts" to the attention of the person on the street.

E. THE PRESUPPOSITION OF PROPOSITIONAL TRUTH

Can truth be captured in a statement which then is "the truth"? After all, two plus two equals four. But I have never seen a "two" or a "four." Numbers belong to the unreal world of mathematics. In the real world we live in, life is historical and truth is historical. This does not mean that truth does not exist or is not truth. It does mean that even a proposition such as "God is one" must be understood as an historical proposition (see Jas 2:19). Who is God in this statement? What are the actions of this God? Furthermore, what is "one" in this context? Is it one over against the many? How does this fit in with Christian language about God being triune? What is at stake here is not a kind of new math, but what it means to be human, to be historical.

In times past theologians did hold that truth in religion could be stated in propositions and that the Bible contained propositions which Christians should hold to as the truth. That was because of the prevailing philosophy of the time, a philosophy built on a static, logical view of truth. But the Bible is not tied to any particular philosophy or any particular philosophical view of truth. For Christians truth is a person (see Jn 14:6) whom we know by faith. Truth is therefore dynamic, personal, relational, historical. Today the presupposition of propositional truth belongs largely to a bygone era. Even sentences that are propositions often communicate more by what they evoke than by what they denote logically. Thus the historical-critical method with its dynamic, historical view of truth and propositions is not a threat but a help in understanding what the Bible means for you and me.

A Lutheran Approach

Fortunately no one is saved by the correct interpretation of Scripture, or none of us would be saved. We are saved by Jesus Christ. Nevertheless we need to discern who it is we believe in. How can we discern? What is the final authority? The Bible is the final authority, of course. The problem is that the Bible must be interpreted, for it must speak to all time as well as to its time. Who can authoritatively interpret the Bible? Is it satisfactory to say that the Bible is simply to be taken as it is because it is inerrant? But those who do this disagree widely among themselves. Is it satisfactory to say that the church is to interpret the Bible? But there is no "church" to which all churches grant such authority. Nor can the matter be left to individuals, for they go their own ways. Lutherans propose a theological answer. Basic to Lutheran understanding is that the word of God is to be understood in three senses, in descending order of importance. First of all, the Word of God is Jesus Christ (see Jn 1:1–14). Second, the word of God is the preached word, the living voice of the gospel. Third, the word of God is the written word, the text of Scripture.

FIVE LUTHERAN PRINCIPLES FOR INTERPRETING SCRIPTURE

1. The New Testament interprets the Old. In other words, the two Testaments are not equal. Not only is the New Testament that which came later and therefore interprets the Old, but also the New Testament brings something new, Jesus Christ. Not only does the New Testament fulfill the Old, and therefore the Old Testament is to be taken very seriously, but the New Testament brings that which the Old Testament does not have, the cross and resurrection. The Old Testament, to be sure, describes the sufferings of Job, the suffering servant of Isaiah 53, and Jeremiah, but these are not to be compared with God's Son dying on the cross in the New Testament. For this reason those whose faith is centered in the death and resurrection of Jesus Christ interpret the Old Testament through the New.

2. The clear interprets the unclear. The converse is not true; the unclear does not interpret the clear. First of all, the interpreter is not to begin with difficult passages, such as 1 Samuel 2:6: "The Lord kills and brings to life," or 1 Corinthians 15:29: "What do people mean by being baptized on behalf of the dead?" Instead, the interpreter must begin with clear passages describing how God has acted and the human predicament; then it is possible to place difficult passages in their proper context. But another step is involved beyond historical and intellectual clarity,

for in the second place, clarity is that which points to Christ, and whatever does not point to Christ is unclear. In other words, clarity is internal, theological, and not historical or intellectual. At times Luther did, to be sure, argue for the external clarity of Scripture, but that was in order to defend himself against his opponents. True clarity, however, is found only in Christ.

3. Scripture interprets itself. But does this not mean that one is arguing in a circle? Does this mean that one cannot use other material to help understand Scripture? To the contrary. Every possible tool needs to be used in order to understand what Scripture has to say. Nor is Scripture understood therefore to be a perfect system, containing all knowledge and truth. What is meant is that Scripture is the final authority and cannot be subsumed under or judged by any other authority. Yet such finality is not finality in a wooden sense. Scripture is the final authority because it points to Christ, and nothing can be allowed to be a higher authority. Christ is the one who gives Scripture whatever authority it has.

4. *Was Christum treibet.* No satisfactory translation into English exists. Literally the words mean: "What drives Christ." What is meant is that what "promotes" Christ is the truth, that where one finds Christ, there is the truth. This may seem to be simply another slogan, like "Christ alone," yet it expresses in a profound sense the heart of the Lutheran approach to Scripture.

5. Interpreting Scripture can only be done within the church. This may sound intolerant. And it does not solve the question where "the" church is. Again, what is meant is that Christ is found in and through his church, and that it is in the church that his Spirit is working. A person might speculate about whether Christ and his Spirit are present outside of the church, and if so, the definition of the church would need to be broadened or what it means for Christ and his Spirit to be present might need to be redefined. All such speculation remains pure speculation. What the Christian knows for sure is that Christ and

his Spirit are present within his church and that those who are outside of Christ are, because they lack his Spirit, unable to interpret Christ correctly and therefore unable to interpret Scripture correctly.

It is obvious that all five Lutheran principles really state the same thing, that where one finds Christ, there one finds the truth, and that this is how Scripture is to be interpreted. Finally this is a theological judgment. As a consequence, Lutherans not only have no problem with the historical-critical method but use it gladly when it helps point to Christ and question the method and its results when it does not point to Christ.

The reader will object. Is it not impossible to believe in the "who," Jesus Christ, without also believing in the "what" about what he did and what he means for you and me? Is not therefore the historical-critical method to be rejected because it calls into question or may seem to call into question some or all of the "what"?

Lutherans take the "what" very seriously. As is well known, Lutherans take Scripture very seriously. They also take Christian tradition very seriously. Three ecumenical creeds, the Apostles' Creed, the Nicene Creed, and the Athanasian Creed, are all part of the beginning of the Lutheran confessional book, the *Book of Concord*. The *Book of Concord* is very specific about the "what" of the Christian faith and is, furthermore, full of references to the so-called church Fathers of the Christian tradition. Finally, however, for Lutherans the question is "how" the "what" is used. Commitment to the "what" by itself could be an historical faith that has nothing to do with salvation. Christian faith is not only or primarily philosophical or historical truth. The important question is "how" such faith is part of a person's life.

When Lutherans spell out this stance, they normally use five slogans. Each of these slogans is like a miniature credal statement.

1. Christ alone. Christ is the sole foundation, "the way, the truth, and the life" (Jn 14:6). Thus "the truth" is an historical person of a particular time and place, who did certain things and said certain things. Yet he is "the truth" who determines what all other truth is.

The difficulty is that although everyone agrees that Christ is "the truth," very different views of Christ remain. "Christ alone" remains a hollow formula. Nor is anything changed by holding that "the gospel" is the truth, for "the gospel," like "Christ alone," remains a hollow formula that has been filled with varying content. Therefore the alternatives are either to identify truth and gospel with the whole book called the Bible or to try to find some way to sort out the different views of Christ and gospel. No matter how much some claim to take the first of the alternatives, everyone in fact operates on the basis of the second.

2. Grace alone. No one denies that salvation is by "grace alone." But what does this mean? Is grace truly "alone" or does it include works? What about the law? Is grace to be categorized variously, as natural grace, actual grace, prevenient grace, and the like? Because of these difficulties, Lutherans make use of the Pauline phrase "justification of the ungodly" (Rom 4:5) so that grace truly remains grace and sin truly remains sin. Arguments remain, to be sure, about the "law" and "works" and "rewards," but the basic thrust of the Lutheran stance is made clear by the Pauline phrase, "justification of the ungodly." Yet more must be said.

3. Faith alone. All may agree on "grace alone," but few agree on "faith alone." Is there nothing else except "faith alone"? Do no works apply? Yes, the Christian has no guarantees as the world reckons guarantees, for all experience including the experience of faith itself is ambiguous. Faith is based upon God's faithfulness to his promise in Jesus Christ, not on any security a person might find in the experience of faith or any other expe-

rience. Since through the promise a person is free from all demands of the law, a new world begins, a joyful life freely doing
what others need.

4. Cross alone. Lutheran theology is cross-centered. The
cross, symbol of torture and defeat, is the power of God for salvation (see 1 Cor 1:22–24). The cross without the resurrection is
simply a tragedy. Conversely, the resurrection without the cross
is simply a fantasy. Both cross and resurrection must be held as a
unity. Yet as long as Christians continue in this world, their lives
continue to be lives under the cross, broken by sin, sickness,
weakness, and death.

5. Scripture alone. Would this be the place where Lutherans
finally establish the "what" in some other way than by means of
"theology"? Not at all. "Scripture alone" does not mean that
Scripture in all its parts is equally valid. Precisely because Lutherans take Scripture seriously and in its literal sense, they take
the difficulties in Scripture seriously, whether brought to their
attention by the historical-critical method or by any other means.
But Christ is the truth, not the difficulties.

Why should these five Lutheran slogans, all stating "Christ is
the truth," be thought to be authoritative for the Christian faith?
Could not other slogans, such as "the church alone" or "inerrancy
alone," be used just as well? And have not Lutherans with these
five slogans tied themselves to "what" instead of "how" after all?
But when Lutherans spell out their stance, they take one final
step.

Final authority lies in the proclamation of the promise. To
put it another way, when Lutherans are asked about the "what,"
their proper answer is to proclaim the promise that for Christ's
sake all your sins are forgiven. The reason for doing this is that
the question of authority is but the symptom of a deeper question, sin, and the answer is to proclaim the promise to you, not to
present you with "what" that supersedes all other "whats." And if

you ask why this promise, the Lutheran will proclaim the promise to you once again. It is in the proper use of the promise that final authority lies; this is the "how." Final authority lies in the fact that through the Holy Spirit the promises are self-authenticating. As children Lutherans used to memorize Luther's explanation to the third article of the Apostles' Creed: "I believe that I cannot by my own reason or understanding believe in Jesus Christ my Lord or come to him, but the Holy Spirit has called me through the gospel. . . ."

For all of these reasons Lutherans do not reject the historical-critical method. Moreover, a person cannot escape this method, because it belongs to the very air we breathe in this century. It can help us better understand ourselves and Scripture. At the same time Lutherans are aware of the fact that the historical-critical method is itself historical and must be examined critically. Finally whatever points to Christ is the truth, and what is needed is that the promise of salvation in Jesus Christ be proclaimed.

EPHESIANS

Almost nothing hints at a concrete setting for the letter. Most satisfactory is the thesis that the original actually stated "in Ephesus" and that the copyists for some of the oldest and weightiest manuscripts, knowing that the contents of the letter do not match what the Book of Acts says about Paul and perhaps hoping to transform the letter into a letter for the whole church, simply omitted the destination.

Did Paul write the letter to the Ephesians? The first and most telling reason for holding that Paul did not write Ephesians is the close relationship between Ephesians and Colossians. Larger patterns within the two letters are conspicuously similar. Most decisive is the use of similar terminology but in a different sense. Which letter was written first? Colossians has to have been first because it deals with a concrete situation. The author of Ephesians abstracted from that situation. It is difficult to imagine how the opposite sequence might have happened.

The second reason for holding that Paul did not write Ephesians is theological. More specifically, the church for Paul can be either the local congregation or the universal church. He does, to be sure, think it important to agree with the mother church in Jerusalem and twice writes of the church as a whole (1 Cor 15:9; Gal 1:13). Yet in Ephesians the church always is the universal church. According to Paul it is better not to marry because the end is near, although those who are married should stay as they are and those who lack self-control ought to marry (1 Cor 7). Ephesians paints an entirely different picture of marriage. It is to be a reflection of the perfect unity which exists between Christ and his bride, the church (5:22–33).

The final reason for holding that Paul did not write Ephesians is stylistic. What stands out most of all is the lavish use of words; a freshman English teacher would say the style is redundant.

Taken individually none of the reasons against Pauline authorship may seem overpowering, but the cumulative weight of evidence becomes conclusive. Who then wrote the letter to the Ephesians? He was someone well acquainted with Paul's teaching and probably, because of his literary style and knowledge of Jewish tradition, a Jewish-Christian. More than that one cannot say. When was the letter written? Since Ephesians is dependent on Colossians and familiar with most of Paul's other letters, the earliest date is probably A.D. 80. Ignatius of Antioch, martyred shortly after A.D. 110, seems to be familiar with Ephesians (Eph 12:2; see Pol 5:1), which would set the upper limit.

Externally Ephesians has the form of a letter, with a proper opening, thanksgiving/blessing, intercession, body, and closing. In actual fact Ephesians is hardly a letter at all, for it is too general and theological. At the same time it is quite specific, aimed at mature Christians who are being asked to remember what their baptism means for the church and their life in Christ. The best way to categorize Ephesians is to call it a liturgical discourse which has been put in the form of a letter.

Ephesians 2:1–10

At first glance this section might seem to be a break in the thanksgiving/intercession which began in 1:15 and continues in 3:1, 14. Yet the overriding theme of God's action in Christ continues, as can be seen by the way what is stated in 1:20 is applied to the Christian in 2:5–6. Redemption and forgiveness, mentioned in 1:7, is the theme of the first section of the second chapter, while reuniting all things (1:10; see 1:23) is the theme of the second section, and 2:19–22 picks up the theme of the church in 1:23.

The structure of this section, and for that matter the whole chapter, is also based on the pattern "once—but now," found in succinct form in 5:8 but here spanning many verses. In modern America this pattern exists as well. We find it, for example, in the line "I once was lost but now am found" from the hymn "Amazing Grace." In New Testament times it is used in Romans 6:17–22, Galatians 4:8–9, Colossians 1:21–22, and 1 Peter 2:10, to cite but a few places. Its purpose is to bring out the contrast between past and present, between being without Christ and being in Christ, and as a consequence it is often connected with baptism. With thankfulness the Christian reflects on the evils of the past and the glorious certainty of his new status; at times an appropriate life in Christ is also mentioned. The words "once—but now" are not required for the pattern, for the contrast by itself is all that is needed. In vv. 2 and 3 the word "once" appears as a clue to the contrast introduced by "but" in v. 4. In v. 5 the contrast lies in the content of the verse. Only in v. 13, after "at one time" (v. 11) and "at that time" (v. 12) have appeared again as clues, do the words "but now" actually appear along with another "once." In v. 19 the contrast again lies in the content of the verse. Nowhere else in the New Testament is this pattern used more frequently.

The Revised Standard Version of the Bible, a translation originally prepared under American Protestant auspices and widely used in Protestant (and some Catholic) churches, contains the following translation of Ephesians 2:1–10:

> [1]And you he made alive, when you were dead through the trespasses and sins [2]in which you once walked, following the course of this world, following the prince of the power of the air, the spirit that is now at work in the sons of disobedience. [3]Among these we all once lived in the passions of our flesh, following the desires of body and mind, and so we were by nature children of wrath, like the rest of mankind. [4]But God, who is rich in mercy, out of the great love with which he loved us, [5]even when we were dead through our trespasses, made us alive together with Christ (by grace you have been saved), [6]and raised us up with him, and made us sit with him in the heavenly places in Christ Jesus, [7]that in the coming ages he might show the immeasurable riches of his grace in kindness toward us in Christ Jesus. [8]For by grace you have been saved through faith; and this is not your own doing, it is the gift of God—[9]not because of works, lest any man should boast. [10]For we are his workmanship, created in Christ Jesus for good works, which God prepared beforehand, that we should walk in them.

The first seven verses are one long sentence, and the verb "made alive" does not occur until v. 5. "Walking" according to the flesh (vv. 2–3) is the first half of a parenthesis that is closed by the "walk" according to good works in v. 10. The first seven verses state the problem, which is sin, and the solution, which is God's action. The final three verses sum up what salvation by grace means, although a parenthetical slogan in v. 5 anticipates the summary.

1. "And" is simply a connective. "Dead" refers, of course, to spiritual death, which is the most serious kind of death possible because it means being cut off from God. The cause of death is "trespasses and sins." No distinction should be drawn between these two terms, which both by the fact that two are used and that they are plural express the totality of sin. According to Paul's theology, sin brings about death (Rom 5:12, 21; 6:23; 1 Cor 15:56); he is referring, however, first of all to physical death. Nothing indicates that "you" is a reference to Gentile Christians. Rather, this is a description of the predicament which includes all, and "you" would normally be used in a letter at this point. The RSV has supplied the verb "he made alive" from v. 5.

2. Three names, which are really the same name, are given for the evil force which opposes God. The first has been translated as "the course of this world" by the RSV. The phrase actually describes Aion, the god of this age, who according to the syncretistic thought of the Hellenistic world ruled all of space and time. "This world" stands in opposition to the "coming world" that God will rule. Another name for the evil one is "the prince of the power of the air." As in Colossians 1:13, "power" does not mean a quality but the sphere that the "prince" rules. The "air" is the lowest level of the heavens; human beings reach up into this level, for they either battle against evil (6:11–12) or are subject to it, as in this verse. The "spirit" is simply a general name for the same evil force. Each of the three names describes the totality of evil (see 1:21; 6:11, 16). This is the evil force that is "now" at work among the disobedient ones, leading them through sin to death (v. 1). Thus by implication evil is not "now" at work among Christians and consequently they are free from its rule.

3. A change is made to "we." Nothing indicates that Jewish Christians are meant, as some have claimed in order to support

the thesis that in v. 1 "you" refers to Gentile Christians. "We all" is a shift to the inclusive style used in confession; we all confess that we are subject to sin, death, and evil. In addition, "we" anticipates the use of "we" and "us" in the following verses and may reflect Colossians 2:13. "Lived" more consciously describes life together (2 Cor 1:12; 1 Tim 3:15), while "walked" (v. 2) tends to be more individualistic (see 5:2, 8, 15). Only here in Ephesians does "flesh" have the negative sense it does in Paul. "Passions" and "desires" point to the abundance and completeness of sin, just as "body and mind," which could be translated as "flesh and evil thought," is the whole man in opposition to God. Radical sin in v. 3 produces an effective contrast to radical grace in v. 4. The concluding part of this verse has been one of the classical proof texts for the doctrine of original sin. Unfortunately the RSV has added "so," as if a conclusion were being drawn which could be considered a general principle, when in matter of fact this clause is parallel to the earlier part of the verse. What is meant is that since we too were dead in our trespasses and sins and enslaved to the prince of this world, we too were children of wrath like the sons of disobedience. "By nature" should therefore be translated as "really" or "totally" (see Gal 4:8; Wis 13:1). "Wrath" stands in contrast to mercy in v. 4 (see 5:6).

4. "But now God has acted" is what the beginning of this verse intends, for the "once—but now" pattern applies here. The basis of God's action is his mercy, which is mentioned in 1 Peter 1:3 and Titus 3:5 in connection with baptism. Thus here also baptism probably should be understood. God's predestining love has already been set forth in 1:5 and Christ's very concrete love for the church will be described later (see 5:2, 25). In v. 5 the words "were dead through the trespasses" are repeated from v. 1 in order to bring out once again the contrast between our problem and God's solution. The shift back and forth between "we" and "you" in this verse and in vv. 8–10 demonstrates that the au-

thor did not write at one point to Gentile Christians and at another to Jewish Christians. Such a hypothesis would become extremely complicated in this section! Instead the author made use of traditional slogans and materials which he did not follow slavishly, making it difficult for us today to determine exactly what is traditional and what is adaptation.

5-6. That we were "made alive together with Christ" begins to apply 1:20 to us. Colossians 2:13 is clearly parallel to this passage. When were we made alive? The aorist tense points to a specific time in the past, which the parallel in Colossians 2:11–13 shows to be baptism. Paul would have written that we have been buried with Christ and that we shall be made alive and raised and made to sit at the right hand, but here nothing has been reserved for the future (see Rom 6:8; 8:11; 1 Cor 15:22, 52; Phil 3:9–11). This is very close to realized eschatology. It cannot be lightly dismissed as mere rhetoric occasioned by the enthusiastic joy that baptism evokes or as simply the description of Christ, the representative of the new humanity, already sitting in the heavenly places. The author fully intended to state that salvation is complete, even though, as in 1:14, he qualified his position and did not fall into the heresy condemned in 2 Timothy 2:18 or into Gnosticism.

In the middle of things the author adds a parenthesis that anticipates v. 8: "by grace you have been saved." The verb is in the perfect tense, indicating that salvation took place in the past and continues into the present. Paul did not use the verb "to save" in the past tense except for Romans 3:24, where the aorist indicating an event in the past is kept in balance by the future reference of the phrase "in this hope"; for him "to save" refers to those who are in the process of being saved yet will be saved at the last judgment (1 Cor 15:2; 2 Cor 6:2) and to future salvation (Rom 5:9–10; 13:11; 1 Thess 5:8–9). Understanding grace as the principle of salvation is very similar to what is stated in Romans 3:24, where Paul adapted earlier materials with a liturgical background, just as the author of Ephesians at this point adapted liturgical materials.

That we "sit with him in the heavenly places" is one of several very striking examples of how the author of Ephesians tends to think in terms of space instead of time. Even the pattern "once—but now" is really a description of two opposing spheres rather than progress across time. At times Paul did, to be sure, use space categories (for example, Rom 10:6; 1 Cor 15:47; Phil 3:20; 1 Thess 4:16), although he preferred time categories and occasionally a space category will also have a future reference (see 1 Thess 4:16). But in the letter to the Ephesians space categories have a decisive place, as in 1:3, 20–22; 3:19; 4:9–10, 15–16, and this passage.

7. In spite of his preference the author of Ephesians, like Paul, used both categories. "In the coming ages" refers to the future. Tempting as it might be to understand the "ages" as personal evil forces in analogy to the "Aion of this world" in v. 2, elsewhere in this letter the plural has a purely temporal meaning (3:9, 11, 21). The plural form by this time had become customary through use in doxologies and simply meant "all times." Thus v. 7 means that in all future times God will effectively "show" (see 1:9) the "riches of his grace" (see 1:7) to us in Christ. Yet this verse must not be understood apart from 1:21 and the fact that Christ already rules the "coming ages."

8–9. The parenthesis from v. 5 now develops into a short summary of Pauline theology. The summary is made up of Pauline slogans and as in v. 5 seems to echo the same sort of materials Paul used in Romans 3:24. The sovereignty of God's grace could hardly be confessed with greater clarity. But even though "grace alone" and "faith alone" are present, "saved" is once again as in v. 5 in the perfect tense. Paul's eschatological dialectic of justification is absent where it is hard to imagine that Paul himself would have omitted it. Two "not" phrases define what grace is: "not of ourselves," "not of works." Paul's polemic against the works of the law is nowhere implied. Where Paul spoke only of "works," his polemic was always implied (see Rom 4:2, 6; 9:32; 11:6). Ephesians 2:9, however, simply counterposes grace and every human work. Paul frequently warned against "boasting" (Rom 4:2; 1 Cor 1:28–31; 4:7; Phil 3:3), which in its most insidious form is the claim to be better than others, so that grace is still not sovereign.

10. In this context to be "created" is the same as what Paul meant by becoming God's "new creation" (2 Cor 5:17; Gal 6:15; Eph 4:24). When did this new creation take place? Baptism could be meant (see Col 3:9–10; Eph 4:24), yet in addition before the foundation of the world God "destined us to be his sons" and to be "holy and blameless" (1:4–5, 11–12). In no way does this passage mean that Christians have been prepared to do good works, for it is the "good works" that have been prepared beforehand. But Christians will "walk" the way of good works because of freedom and gratitude, not because of an attempt to save themselves (see Rom 1:5; 6:16–18; Phil 2:12–13). That Christians "should" walk the way of good works is also intended by the author.

SUMMARY

Lutherans understand the word of God as Jesus Christ, the preached word of the gospel, and the written word of Scripture. The five Lutheran principles for interpreting Scripture are the following: the New Testament interprets the Old; the clear interprets the unclear; Scripture interprets itself; what "promotes" Christ is the truth; interpreting Scripture can only be done within the church. The Lutheran stance is captured in the five "alones"—Christ, grace, faith, the cross, and Scripture.

Has anything important been lost in the translation of Paul's apocalyptic theology of justification by faith into ecclesiological universalism in the letter to the Ephesians? In Ephesians, Christ clearly is central, as is grace. But Paul's eschatological tension betweeen "already" and "not yet" has been greatly lessened. Already "we have redemption" (1:7), already "we sit with him in the heavenly places" (2:6). Therefore the need for ethics and battling the evil one (4:27; 5:6; 6:11–17) has been greatly diminished, in spite of the space these topics are given. The role of the law has become much smaller (2:15). For Paul the law is not simply a Jewish issue, but plays a decisive role in evaluating who one really is before God. The law, in fact, is a key to the polemic function of justification by faith. Ephesians is, of course, written in a different time and situation. The question is whether anything essential for Paul's theology has been lost when judgment and the law have lost much of their significance.

To put it another way: something has changed in Ephesians. The church has become determinative, and justification by faith takes second place. Is it important if the basic christological emphasis of justification by faith is lessened or even lost? Lutherans and those in the Reformation tradition have claimed that justification by faith is central and have been unwilling to allow ecclesiology to determine Christology.

Recommended Readings

James Barr, *The Bible in the Modern World* (New York-Evanston-San Francisco-London: Harper & Row, 1973). A challenge by a competent Old Testament scholar to all those who want to take the Bible seriously. The basic questions are raised.

Heinrich Bornkamm, *Luther and the Old Testament,* tr. E. and R. Gritsch (Philadelphia: Fortress, 1969). Technical and already an older book, this is an important contribution to the discussion of Luther's use of Scripture.

Roland E. Clements, *One Hundred Years of Old Testament Interpretation* (Philadelphia: Westminster Press, 1976). For the beginning student this is a helpful step into the discussion of Old Testament interpretation.

Ellen Flessmann-van Leer, *The Bible. Its Authority and Interpretation in the Ecumenical Movement* (Faith and Order Paper No. 99; Geneva: World Council of Churches, 1979). A collection of the documents and as such very helpful.

The Function of Doctrine and Theology in Light of the Unity of the Church (New York: Lutheran Council in the USA, 1978). A highly technical but useful debate among Lutherans is laid out in this volume.

Edgar Krentz, *The Historical-Critical Method* (Philadelphia: Fortress, 1975). The best short summary of what the historical-critical method is really about.

Werner Georg Kümmel, *The New Testament: The History of the Investigation of Its Problems*, tr. S. Gilmour and H. Kee (Nashville/New York: Abingdon Press, 1972). The classic history and summary of what has happened to the New Testament in the last centuries.

John Reumann (ed.), in collaboration with Samuel H. Nafzger and Harold H. Ditmanson, *Studies in Lutheran Hermeneutics* (Philadelphia: Fortress, 1979). A modern debate among Lutherans about interpretation and Scripture.

Peter Stuhlmacher, *Historical Criticism and Theological Interpretation of Scripture*, tr. R. Harrisville (Philadelphia: Fortress, 1977). A recent attempt by a Lutheran to establish a more moderating discussion of historical criticism.

Theological Professors of the American Lutheran Church, *The Bible: Book of Faith* (Minneapolis: Augsburg Publishing House, 1964). A popular volume but very useful for those who are facing historical criticism for the first time.

Daniel J. Harrington, S.J.

Conclusion: Convergence and Divergence

This little book has covered a great deal of ground. After a sketch of the history of biblical interpretation in the church, it has provided explanations of how the Bible is understood today in the Catholic, evangelical, and Lutheran traditions. Even though the authors do not claim to be official spokesmen for their traditions, they have tried to reflect in a concise and straightforward way how Catholic, evangelical, and Lutheran biblical scholars work. My concluding remarks will try to highlight some of the major points of convergence and divergence.

The most obvious point of convergence is that in all three traditions intelligent and well-trained scholars are studying the same basic collection of books (at least in the case of the New Testament) in basically the same ways. They come to the biblical text because they (and their church traditions) believe that study of the Bible will enable them to understand better the mystery of God's revelation in Christ. In their study they use the same set of intellectual tools. Since the books of the Bible are pieces of literature, modern biblical scholars make literary criticism their starting point, especially with regard to literary genre and context. Much of their energy goes into clarifying the historical setting of

the books of the Bible with the help of language study, archaeology, and general history. These scholars are sensitive to the traditional character of the biblical material through their use of
form, source, and redaction criticisms. Many are cautious about
the philosophical claim of some radical historians that reason is
the ultimate interpreter of the biblical text. Almost all frankly admit the presence of theological diversity within the canon, but
they are divided about whether there is a fundamental unity in
the Bible and what constitutes it. Nearly all assume that the results of their biblical study bear on church life today.

The task of biblical scholarship in all three traditions is first
and foremost the meaning of the biblical text in its original historical setting. Recognizing the theoretical problems involved in
bridging the historical gap of two thousand years and in determining the intention of any author, modern biblical scholars
make every effort to come as close as possible to the original
meaning in its historical context. These modern biblical scholars
work in a variety of settings. Some are monks; some are professors; some are preachers. Some are all three.

What distinguishes modern biblical scholars from their
predecessors is the dramatically larger fund of historical resources that can aid them in approaching their goal of elucidating the original meaning of the text. The ancient texts discovered
in the past century or so, the understanding of the material culture of antiquity through archaeological excavations, the tech-
nological advances made in disseminating information—all these
can contribute to a better appreciation of the original meaning of
the biblical text than could have been gained by Augustine,
Thomas Aquinas, Erasmus, or Luther. This is not to claim that
any modern biblical scholar is the intellectual or spiritual superior of these great interpreters of the past. I am merely suggest-
ing that progress has been made and continues to be made in
grasping what the biblical writers sought to communicate to their
first readers.

The ways in which modern biblical scholars present the results of their study indicate that they themselves perceive some important ecumenical convergence. In addition to writing for their own ecclesial constituencies, they are conscious of participating in an interconfessional and international dialogue. This shows itself in the congresses and meetings that they attend regularly, the series and journals in which they publish their research, and the books and articles that they read and cite in their own works.

However important and encouraging this convergence among Catholic, evangelical, and Lutheran biblical scholars may be, there is also considerable divergence. This divergence is rooted mainly in the historical settings of the interpreters, some theological questions of long-standing significance, and the process of interpretation itself. Most of these sources of divergence are on the edge of, or even beyond the boundaries of, modern biblical study, and so they are chiefly treated by systematic theologians. Nevertheless, attention to them does much to explain why serious divergence still exists among Catholic, evangelical, and Lutheran biblical scholars.

The first source of divergence concerns the historical settings of the interpreters. The liberation theologians have made us all more sensitive to the interpreter's setting as a factor in interpretation. Catholic scholars can no more deny their church's ambivalence regarding biblical scholarship in the past than evangelicals can put aside the revivalist and fundamentalist impulses of their religious tradition or Lutherans can ignore the Scholasticism that quickly surrounded some of Luther's more explosive theological ideas. Neither can modern biblical scholars escape entirely the epistemological assumptions that still shape their traditions: the moderate realism of Catholic Scholasticism, the Common Sense Realism of the American fundamentalists, and the varied philosophical perspectives of at least some German Lutherans. Moreover, the way in which "church" is understood differs from group to group: the hierarchical structure of official Catholicism, the diverse and sometime volatile local communities of evangelicalism, and the Lutheran emphasis on the gospel's challenge to all visible church structures.

The second source of divergence is theology. The essays in this book have called attention to the controversies today that surround revelation (propositional versus personal), inspiration, inerrancy, and the authority of Scripture. These are serious theological issues with very long and complicated histories. They are frustrating and elusive. They tend to generate abstractions and polemics. But they will not go away. And they do have an impact on biblical interpretation, since what interpreters hold about the nature of the Bible (the church's book, the word of God, or the place in which the gospel may be encountered) will surely affect the way that they interpret it.

These essays have also raised the theological problem of the unity and diversity within the canon of Scripture. The question here is: What does one do with the diverse theological voices within the canon? Lutherans often follow Luther's lead in using Paul's letters to the Romans and the Galatians, the fourth gospel, and 1 Peter as a kind of "canon within the canon" to judge the correctness and value of the other books (*was Christum treibet*). Catholics try to hold the whole canon together with their reliance on the living church and its magisterium as the official interpreter of Scripture. Evangelicals work away at resolving the apparent contradictions and tensions within Scripture on the assumption that it is all the word of God. These divergent approaches to the problem of the different voices in the canon of Scripture are rooted in differing approaches to the significance of ongoing Christian history: the progressive unfolding of the divine plan (Catholicism), the return to Christian origins (evangelicals), and the dialectical relationship between the gospel and history (Lutheranism).

The third source of divergence involves the process of interpretation itself, especially as the interpreter tries to articulate the significance of the biblical text for the church today. If one grants the possibility of understanding today the meaning of the biblical text in its original setting, there is some debate about what really has been achieved for people today. Surely a better historical knowledge has been gained. But Professor Hagen's question remains: Did the historical-critical method win any new or better or clearer understanding of the text that was unavailable to Augustine, Thomas Aquinas, Luther, or Calvin? I would say "yes" in reply, but many people would not. Then there is the very difficult problem of distinguishing between the "cultural" and the "normative" elements in the Bible. All church groups do this kind of distinguishing, whether we call the normative elements the "gospel" (Lutherans), the "word of God" (evangelicals), or "divine revelation" (Catholics). But how we do it and what criteria we use in doing it are seldom made clear. Finally there is the fact that the Bible is being read and interpreted by people all over the world, and it is being used to respond to very diverse concerns (rich and poor, first world and third world, post-Enlightenment cultures and other cultures). The kind of historical criticism outlined by the three exegetes in this book is deeply rooted in Western European and North American culture, and some third world scholars are vigorous in taking us to task for our cultural narrowness.

Much convergence and much divergence—that seems to be the state of biblical interpretation today among Catholic, evangelical, and Lutheran exegetes today. The convergence stems mainly from the fact that these exegetes are working at the same texts and in the same basic ways. The divergence arises largely from the different historical settings in which these interpreters work, some very serious theological problems, and the process of interpretation itself.